ON BEING HUMAN

ON BEING HUMAN

BY

PAUL ELMER MORE

NEW SHELBURNE ESSAYS

VOLUME III

Essay Index Reprint Series

BOOKS FOR LIBRARIES PRESS

FREEPORT, NEW YORK

CONTENTS

CONTENTS

A REVIVAL OF HUMANISM

[Published in *The Bookman* for March 1930]

UNDER the editorial supervision of Professor Norman Foerster, assisted by three other scholars, a group of fifteen writers have contributed to make a volume of essays under the collective title of *Humanism and America*.[1] With a few exceptions the contributors range in age from thirty to forty-five years, being young enough to speak for the coming generation and old enough to have passed the first inexperience of youth. Some of the younger men have already made their mark in the critical contentions of the past four or five years; others will be scarcely known to the public. Inevitably the papers are not of equal weight and interest, but the high average of intelligence is heartening and, if it may be said without offence, a little surprising. As a whole the book seems to me, in its field, about the most significant event that has fallen under my notice in many years of reading and reviewing. I may say this without hesitation, because, though parts of an essay are reprinted from a recent publication of my own, I have written nothing for the volume, and my share in determining its character is altogether negligible.

[1] *Humanism and America*, edited by Norman Foerster. Farrar & Rinehart. $3.50. [A complete list of the contributors with the titles of their articles will be found at the conclusion of this essay.]

Mr. Foerster calls attention to the fact that the contributors, though writing quite independently one of the other, "agree in certain broad, fundamental opinions"; and I have thought that I could not better serve the cause, of which the present work may be regarded as a spirited manifesto, than by pointing out what these common opinions are and by attempting to show the significance of the divergence where this begins.

I

On one point the agreement is already complete. From the first sentence of the preface provided by the editor to the concluding essay on "Courage and Education" by a senior student at Bowdoin College, one note is sounded over and over again: "The noise and whirl increase, the disillusion and depression deepen, the nightmare of Futility stalks before us." Futility is the final word: the literature and art most characteristic of the day are criticized as chaotic, joyless, devoid of beauty, comfortless, fretfully original or feebly conventional, impotent, futile. The blackness of the picture may be somewhat overlaid, as is the wont with those who are confessedly crying for reform; but no great movement for bettering conditions was ever carried to success without a clear sense of wrong to be righted, no hope for the future was ever effective until the bubble of self-complacency was pricked. Conceit of the present is the most deadly bondage of the human spirit, and against this devastating conceit the revolt of so many enlightened minds among the generation just reaching maturity is a sign of the times that may well challenge the attention of those who are still wavering in their allegiance to one side or the other. They may see that the best way to be modern is to break away from the fetters of "modernism."

On another point our humanists are well agreed: they all perceive, and more or less explicitly declare, that the present confusion in letters is connected with a similar confusion in our ideas of life. They see that as we live, so shall we paint and write, or that, as Plato would put it, as we paint and write, so shall we come to live. They might give different answers to the question whether, in the large innovations of time, art precedes in moulding life or life in moulding art; they would all admit, I think, that the two are mutually interactive, and that there can be no great and simple and sincere art without ideals of greatness and simplicity and sincerity prevailing in society. Handsome is that handsome does. Perhaps the finest expression of this rather obvious truth comes to us in the present volume from one whose subtleties of sympathy have not always in the past led him to speak so uncompromisingly, to the effect that "to understand any nobly conceived work of art, one must have lived nobly in deed, in imagination, or in both." Mr. Mather for the moment is thinking rather of the appreciator of art than of the creator, but his maxim, as I am sure he would admit, merely repeats and extends the famous, and sometimes disputed, saying of Longinus, that "sublimity is the echo of a great soul."[2] In this

---

[2] Longinus was not contradicting himself when he wrote: "I feel almost absolved from the necessity of premising at any length that sublimity is a certain distinction and excellence in expression, and that it is from no other source than this that the greatest

spirit Mr. Mather continues (and I wish I could quote
at greater length) :

> . . . appreciation really requires a right and balanced attitude
> towards life. It was really more important for Florence that her
> great citizens, while bowing to the glory that was Greece and the
> grandeur that was Rome, wanted a full and honourable life in
> Florence—it was really more important, I say, that they cared
> discriminatingly for the dignity of their ordinary activities and
> for the authority of their faith, than that they cared *specifically*
> for painting, sculpture, and architecture. In short, some aristo-
> cratic vision of the good life has always been the foundation on
> which great national art has been reared in the past.

That is the note common to all the writers of this
symposium, "the consciousness," as Mr. Stanley P.
Chase expresses it, "of intellectual defeat and spiritual dismay" behind the spasmodic futility of modern
literature. And it is no light matter that this clear
consciousness has made itself felt among a group of
men who (I omit the exceptions) are not old enough
to be open to the charge of decrying the present because it is not their own cherished past, or who, on the
other hand, are not so young as to take delight, like
the puppies of Plato's *Republic,* in the mere act of
tearing things to pieces. They speak, as a body, with
a sobriety of judgement and an earnestness of conviction that must carry weight with any reader not
snared by the Circean flatteries of the present. And it
is to be observed that, up to this point, our militant
critics not only agree among themselves but are also
in accord with those novelists and poets much in the
public eye against whom their challenge of humanism

poets and writers have derived their eminence and gained an im-
mortality of renown." Great art, which is what he means by the
"sublime," would be the noble expression of a noble attitude
towards life.

is intentionally directed. If I understand what is going on in France—and my opinion is confirmed by those who have more knowledge of the subject than I can pretend to—Proust and André Gide and their followers are animated by a determination to face the facts and to make of their art an unflinching record of the intellectual defeat and spiritual dismay they find about them in actual life and within themselves. I have read the same thing of James Joyce, who to the mind of his eulogists is a prophetic voice denouncing the age for its meaningless unrest.

But if harmony reigns between the two camps of humanism and anti-humanism up to this point, beyond it divergence begins and widens. In the first place these novelists and poets of discontent, who are deliberately preying on the intellectual defeat and spiritual dismay of the times, as vultures fatten themselves on carrion, whatever their moral pretext, are in no true sense of the word working for regeneration. They perceive the evil state of society and portray it with gloating contempt. But having no faith in the possible dignity of individual human life, they offer a very dubious alliance to humanism. Rather, on the contrary, they fill their public with a self-congratulating superiority of knowingness, as if to know the sickness about him were sufficient to relieve a man in a hospital of the need of a physician for himself. Where all without exception are depraved, it is a virtue to admit the bitter truth. Thus these apostles of depravity flatter men by degrading mankind; whereas the beginning of humanism, as of religion, is the humility that goes with a sense of personal responsibility.

In the end the distinguishing mark, and largely the cause, of the pessimism of modern literature is a false philosophy. It looks upon human nature with the inflamed vision of a monocular Cyclops, seeing man only as the slave of his temperament, or as a mechanism propelled by complexes and reactions, or as a vortex of sensations, with no will to govern himself, no centre of stability within the flux, no direction of purpose to rise above the influences that carry him hither and thither. At the same time many of these monists are aware that the literature dependent upon such a life has become, like its subject, sicklied with the depression of conscious futility. It is conscience, they say, makes cowards of us all. It is conscience that, unsubdued by all the pleas of a monistic psychology, rebellious to the truths of reason, still invades the unenlightened mind with a sense of futility and remorse. In life the traditional emotions persist in overriding theory; but art is our own to fashion as we will. Let us therefore divorce art from life by exorcizing the phantom of conscience. Then naturalism, being perfect and consistent with itself, will no longer depress its votaries but fill them with the exaltation of liberty. Hence the endeavour in one way or another to dehumanize art by a callous indifference to sentiment which is often confounded with sentimentality, or by the irony of cold contemplation as if the artist, *qua* artist, stood outside of the network of human relations, or by a brutal avowal of irresponsibility, or by a frank revelling in ugliness, or by the glorification of self-expression as a substitute for self-development. Hence too the innumerable treatises now coming from the press, that chatter about the theory of criticism instead of criticizing, as if somehow or other, as art can be detached from life, so criticism can be detached from art. I would not imply that criticism as a means to the appreciation of art may not, for convenience' sake, be isolated from its end and so studied in abstraction; but in many of these works, including the pseudo-scientific treatises of Mr. I. A. Richards, one detects a kind of tacit assumption that if we could perfectly analyse the nature of the instrument, we should be relieved of all worry about the nature of the object for which the instrument is to be used. As if knowledge of the structure of a saw and hammer would make a good carpenter.

Against this monism and its fruits all our militant humanists, if I understand them, are openly or virtually in protest. The question at issue is thus ultimately one of philosophy or psychology. Against those who teach that man is totally submerged in natural law, the humanist lays emphasis on that in man which distinguishes him generically from other animals and so in one part of his composite being lifts him out of the more narrowly defined kingdom of nature; and the humanist assumes for himself this title as opposed to the naturalist because this superadded element, or faculty, however named, is what marks off a man as man. In a word, the humanist is simply one who takes his stand *on being human.* Against those who still hold that man is only a fragmentary cog in the vast machine which we call the universe, moved by the force of some relentless, unvarying, unconscious law, the humanist asserts that we are individual personalities, endowed with the potentiality of free will and answerable for our choice

of good or evil. Against those who reduce man to a
chaos of sensations and instincts and desires checking
and counter-checking one another in endlessly shifting patterns, the humanist points to a separate faculty
of inhibition, the inner check or the *frein vital,* where-
by these expansive impulses may be kept within
bounds and ordered to a design not of their making.
Against those who proclaim that a man can only drift,
like a rudderless ship, with the weltering currents of
change, the humanist maintains that he is capable of
self-direction, and that character, as different from
native temperament, is a growth dependent on clarity
and strength of purpose. Against those who, to ap-
pease the stings of conscience, assure us that we are
what we are by no fault of our own, that, as we have
no responsibility for our character, so the lesson of
wisdom is to shuffle off any sense of regret or remorse
or fear; and against those who go further in flattery
and, through each and every appearance of delin-
quency, assert the instinctive total goodness of unre-
deemed nature—against these the humanist contends
that as free agents we are accountable for defalcations
and aberrations and that self-complacency is the deadliest foe to human excellence. On the other hand, the
humanist will not stand with those who jeer at human
nature, as if men were in no better state than rats
in a trap, rushing distractedly hither and thither, hurl-
ing themselves upon their bars in a pitiable frenzy of
impotence.

In their contention with the naturalists who in one
form or another have for some time dominated the
public mind and controlled the springs of literature,

our rebels argue that their doctrine of humanistic
dualism is no insubstantial web of fancy worn to
veil the hard facts of life, but the outcome of our
surest observation and of our most immediate self-
knowledge. Such a dualism, as Mr. G. R. Elliott
reasons, "is less naïve than the theory of universal
continuity; is better grounded in universal human experience; and, above all, is more truly accordant with
the profound division which any thinking man may
find within himself today when he is sufficiently self-
reliant and experimental to plumb beneath the sur-
faces where our ephemeral psycho-physicisms weave
and flutter." And, replying to those who revolt from
the irrational aspect of dualism, Mr. Elliott continues:

. . . Recently humanism, in its attempt to fulfil and deepen the
experimentality of the modern spirit, has of necessity placed its
chief emphasis upon that inward division. It has insisted that the
opposition between the higher and lower wills within us, whether
they be called "divine" and "natural" or what not, is essentially
inexplicable by expert reason and is nevertheless, from the
present standpoint of human happiness, the most important
feature of the universe arrived at by free and full experimenta-
tion. This humane *dualism* strikes at the very heart of modern
pride, the pride of spiritual *monism*. It sets a true immediacy over
against a false immediacy. It assigns a central value to the
paradox established by the immediate experience of Everyman
when he tries (in the terminology of common sense) to be "at
one with himself" by keeping his "better self" above his "worser
self."

It may seem that the movement I am describing is
essentially negative, with no positive program to offer
in place of the errors it would combat. And it is true
that as matters now stand a good deal of the energy
of its supporters is expended in aggressive protest.
But there are times when it is necessary to demolish
before building, just as it is of no avail to propose a

career of wholesome activity to a sick man until the roots of his disease are eradicated. And there is this to be said in defence of a militant policy: nothing is more likely to draw a group of men together and to prepare them for a concerted advance than the awareness of a common antipathy. The first step in a vigorous campaign must be to distinguish clearly between friend and foe.

Now one certain result of the volume we have under consideration will be to set the contributors and those for whom they speak in sharp contrast not only with the enemies who openly glory in degrading man to the naturalistic level but with those ambiguous flatterers of human nature who more or less speciously claim the title of allies. No excuse remains for muddle-headed critics to compromise the movement by accepting, for example, the saccharine simplicity of that Dr. Charles Francis Potter who recently has acquired a kind of newspaper notoriety (extending, to my knowledge, as far as Lahore, India) by launching a "new religion" of "humanism" wherein humanity is to be enthroned in the place of God, and who, in his initial address, mentioned Mr. Babbitt and myself, among others, as associates in the foundation. The *Commonweal* of October 16, 1929, made the proper reply to such impertinence: "Whoever may have said that man is inherently good, it was certainly not Professor Babbitt; the diverse negators of the supernatural have many names, but that of More is not among them." It is not the least merit of Mr. Babbitt's "Essay at Definition" that it brushes aside the pretensions of a number of usurpers in the field, including M. Sylvain Lévi (who makes Diderot a humanist), Mr.

Lewis Mumford (who performs a like service for Walt Whitman), Mr. F. C. S. Schiller of Oxford (who exalts Protagoras as a humanist above Plato), and that loquacious apostle of sweetness and darkness, Professor John Dewey, and ending with this comment on Mr. Walter Lippmann's *A Preface to Morals:*

. . . he would have us believe that any one who has become disinterested after the scientific fashion has got the equivalent not only of humanism but of "high religion." By thus dissimulating the gap between the wisdom of the ages and the wisdom of the laboratory, he is flattering some of the most dangerous illusions of the present time. He escapes from the main humanitarian tendency to give to feeling a primacy that does not belong to it, only to encourage its other main tendency to accord to physical science a hegemony to which it is not entitled.

In an epoch weltering through a morass of *isms* it is well to know definitely how humanism is opposed to naturalism, and wherein it differs from its presumptive brother, humanitarianism. So much in defence of the aggressive method of warfare employed by the fighting wing of the new movement.

But if humanism has its value as a clear-cut condemnation of certain tendencies always at work in life and literature, though not always so obstreperous as at the present day, it should not be regarded as a mere policy of opposition and obstruction with nothing positive of its own to offer. As a matter of fact it is rather the forces under attack that are open to the charge of negation, and they are under attack for that very reason. Like the naturalist and the humanitarian, the humanist, as Mr. Foerster states in his preface, may take for his creed the saying that the proper study of mankind is man; and he may join with them in adding that the purpose of such study is to enable

mankind to perceive and realize its humanity. But
just here difference makes itself felt. The humanist
is positive in his assertion that the distinguishing
quality of humanity is something overlooked by the
hostile camp. Both would admit that man is the
measure; but it is the naturalist who denies the
existence of that element of man's composite being
which the humanist affirms to be the normal standard
of measurement. Again it is the humanist who takes
into positive account the value of tradition as a complement to the limitations of the individual, and who
regards the present as a small but integral part of the
long experience of the human race. Nor is it true that
he would stifle the creative impulses or smother the
joy of living by the restrictions of a barren discipline.
The law of proportion and measure and the need of
self-restraint are indeed words often on his lips; but
he believes that only by such discipline in the mind
of the artist can the higher creative forces be liberated. He would put a check upon the spasms of eccen-
tricity to the end that the imagination may move
largely in its work of genuine originality.

As between the humanist and the naturalist it is the
former who stands for the great affirmation; it is the
latter who, through obstinate ignorance or in the
name of pseudo-science, limits and contracts and dis-
torts and denies.

II

So far my aim has been to define, I will not say the
new, but the newly advocated, humanism, and to this
end I have endeavoured to bring out the singular and
impressive unanimity among the contributors to the

recently published manifesto. I have not spoken for myself, though it is scarcely necessary to add that I am in entire sympathy with the platform thus expounded. The task has been a pleasant one for me and, I trust, not unprofitable for the reader, for there is a good deal of confusion in the minds of onlookers as to what the movement really signifies and what the battle is all about. It is an old maxim of war, to divide and conquer; and a good many assaults of the enemy would be frustrated if the defenders of the cause did not allow the points on which they differ to create an appearance of discord there where none exists. In what follows I shall speak for myself, though hoping and believing that my opinions will meet with a fair amount of assent. And in so speaking I would insist that nothing I shall say should be taken as a covert retractation of what has preceded, and particularly, if the personal note may here be intruded, that nothing should be interpreted as indicating a rift between myself and my comrade-in-arms of long standing, Mr. Babbitt, in our attitude towards the combined forces of anti-humanism.

The question to be considered is the relation of humanism to religion. Here the reader of Mr. Foerster's miscellany will have observed a divergence of views, although, perhaps for strategical reasons, perhaps in part because of a little uncertainty remaining in the minds of the contributors themselves, the matter has been kept rather in the background. However that may be, by reading between the lines or in some cases by taking into account knowledge otherwise obtained, one becomes aware that the allies are divided into three camps over the issue of religion.

A few would appear to be actually hostile to any belief in the supernatural as essentially anti-humanistic; in one person I know this to be the case, though it would not be guessed from his contribution to the present volume. Others, the majority I suspect, are friendly enough to religion in itself, but either have so vague a conception of its nature and function that practically it fades out of view, or, having clear views of what religion means to life, feel nevertheless that for the regeneration of art the program of humanism is adequate in and of itself. The remainder, some two or three perhaps, hold that without a close alliance between humanism and religion the former is shut off from its chief source of vitality. That is the issue; it cannot be bludgeoned into silence or circumvented.

For my own part, let me admit that to some extent I have been led to revise my earlier position by a number of recent criticisms, ranging from the ignorant and conceited outburst of Mr. Allen Tate on the "Fallacy of Humanism" in the *Criterion* for July 1929, and the *Hound & Horn* for January 1930, to the courteous and thoughtful note on the "High Lights of Humanism" by Mr. George N. Shuster in the *Commonweal* for April 17, 1929. Mr. Tate argues from some vague and indigested "philosophy" which I find difficult to comprehend, whereas Mr. Shuster speaks with the precision of an enlightened Roman Catholic; but they agree in complaining that humanism fails to offer any clear positive basis on which the mind and heart of man may rest. Now from one point of view it would be easy to retort, as I have already attempted to do, that humanism, tested by comparison with its lower rival, has the strength of a great

affirmation; but from another point of view the con-
currence of critics otherwise so contrary-minded—
and I have named only two out of many—has combined with certain questionings from my own inner
experience to compel me to reconsider the whole matter. Something must be wanting to the program of
reform; there is some incompleteness here that explains this common uneasiness of critics so diverse.
What is it? The answer has come to me in two words:
purpose and values. Can humanism, of itself, unaided,
provide the purpose and values it needs for its fulfilment and without which it cannot pass from the
purely critical to the productive state? Must it not for
its driving force depend on religion? The question is
primarily pragmatic, but at the last it involves a whole
philosophy of faith.

Now in one sense humanism takes its stand unhesitatingly on the affirmation of purpose. Its animus
against naturalism is based on the evident fact that the
rejection of free will deprives life of any possibility
of purpose and leaves man a passive victim of chance
or fate. It perceives that a literature depicting our
adventures in such a universe must degenerate into the
clever futilities of an Aldous Huxley or the obscene
rigmarole of a James Joyce, or, seeking to escape the
curse of impotence, into the sadism of a Robinson
Jeffers. But purpose of what? Again the answer is
ready: purpose to put back into life the values of
which a false psychology had emptied it. There is that
in every human being which it behooves him to know
and cherish, a potentiality which it is worth his while
to develop at any cost, a goal of perfection towards
which all his energy should be directed—the high

value of being a man. The program, laid out so long
ago by the great Stagirite, has the ringing appeal of
veracity. It is true, every word of it: yet is it quite
all the truth? The high value of being a man—is that
telos attainable, is it even approachable, without
religion?

The question disquiets me as a humanist. It vexed
Aristotle, and drove him on to make his vast plunge
into the metaphysics of the Absolute. I read him, and
am still disquieted. I turn to my great Aristotelian
friend of the present, from whom I have so often
found help in intellectual difficulties, but in this
matter I am still left unsatisfied. Mr. Babbitt admits
"an element of truth in the assertion of Plato that
things human cannot be properly known without a
previous insight into things divine." He goes further
than this, and accepts the thesis of Pascal to the effect
"that unless man has the support of the supernatural,
unless in short he attains to true humility, he will fall
fatally either into the Stoic pride or else, through the
intermediary stage of scepticism, into the Epicurean
relaxation." He holds that "the humanist will finally
. . . have to take sides in the debate between naturalists and supernaturalists"; and he ranges himself
"unhesitatingly on the side of the supernaturalists."
The language is strong enough. Yet when I try to
grasp what Mr. Babbitt means precisely by the supernatural, I am held at bay by his sweeping reluctance,
veiled perhaps but deeply felt, to associate it with any
kind of "dogmatic or revealed religion." On the other
hand the "religious insight" which he would retain as
an effective background for humanism, leaves me still
asking: insight into what? The attempt to give

"definite content" to this insight by identifying it with
the "higher immediacy" might have satisfied Buddha,
though even that is doubtful; certainly Plato would
not have recognized it as equivalent to his "insight
into things divine," or Pascal as affording "support to
the supernatural." Nor does it seem to me to meet the
clear conviction held by Sophocles or by any other of
the great humanists of ancient Greece.

The cause of humanism is identical, as we have
seen, with belief in free will and purpose as the traits
that distinguish humanity from nature or, if you
prefer, from the rest of nature.[3] And so far the
humanist has no need to call in the sanctions of the
supernatural in the guise of revelation. As Mr. Babbitt puts it with force and finality: "why not affirm
it [man's higher will, or "immortal essence presiding
like a king over his appetites"] first of all as a psychological fact, one of the immediate data of consciousness, a perception so primordial that, compared with
it, the deterministic denials of man's moral freedom
are only a metaphysical dream?" So far the way of
the humanist is clear. But purpose in the direction of
free will implies the realization of values. And here
the difficulties begin. Why should I propose to myself
a line of life which requires a constant exercise of

[3] A certain amount of ambiguity adheres inevitably from historical usage to the words "natural" and "supernatural." One
may, and often does, limit the term "nature" to that which is
common to all animals including man, and designate the distinguishing faculty of man as "supernatural." Or one may, and often
does, speak of that which pertains to man alone as his "higher
nature," while that which man possesses in common with other
animals is called his "lower nature." In this case the "supernatural" will properly designate the other-worldly elements of religion whether known by revelation or by intuition.

choice and restraint, in themselves painful to the natural man, unless something of value is to be attained thereby? Why should I not follow the sway of temperament and satisfy all the desires of nature as they arise? Mr. Babbitt, I know, has an answer to these questions. "In his attempt," he says, "to show the inadequacy of humanism apart from dogmatic and revealed religion, Mr. T. S. Eliot has painted a picture of the humanist exercising in a sort of psychic solitude self-control purely for the sake of control." And against this picture Mr. Babbitt, forgetting, as it seems to me, the full importance of the supernatural already conceded by himself, cites the communion of souls described by Aristotle as attainable on the purely humanistic level by the act of self-control, and upholds worldly happiness as a sufficient guerdon. And Mr. G. R. Elliott (who otherwise stands with Mr. T. S. Eliot for dogmatic and revealed religion, rather than for what may be called just religion) puts the case even more emphatically: "Humanism is the study and practice of the principle of human happiness *uncomplicated* by naturistic dogmas on the one side and religious dogmas on the other."

That blessed word happiness! If only we were sure of attaining it on the human level, how the problem of purpose and value would be simplified! How easy the whole matter would be! Happiness. I cannot forget the terrible ending of *Vanity Fair*: "Ah! *Vanitas Vanitatum!* which of us is happy in this world? Which of us has his desire? or, having it, is satisfied? —come, children, let us shut up the box and the puppets, for our play is played out." And I am haunted by the refrain of so many men who have

drunk deep of the chalice of mortal life and found
always at the bottom the *amari aliquid*: Abd-ar-
Rahman, that great caliph, who at the end counting
up his days could remember only twenty of happiness;
Septimius Severus, master of the world, with his
dying comment, *Omnia fui, et nil expedit*; Solon, with
his famous caution, "Count no man happy until he
is dead"; Socrates, the embodiment of self-control
and good cheer, who, to comfort his friends in the
hour of his condemnation to death, reminded them
that few of our days or nights could equal in happiness a time of deep and dreamless sleep; Johnson,
the sturdy champion of British common sense, denouncing as a liar any man who dared call himself
happy unless drunk; our own Edison, who at least
has reaped all manner of worldly success yet declares
that he has never known a happy man. But there is no
need to multiply random examples. It is always the
same story, whether the word comes from the East
or the West, from the North or the South—always
the bitter truth: In this world we have no abiding
city; he who thinks to find peace in this mortal life
is pursuing a phantom more elusive than the winds.
It may be possible to achieve a kind of simulacrum
of happiness by a dull or bovine acquiescence in things
as they are, or by an indefatigable activity that leaves
no time for reflection, or even by a cunningly managed
pursuit of worldly pleasures; but such a state is pre-
carious always, and at the best devoid of the "high
seriousness" demanded by a genuine humanism.

That is the dilemma that faces the humanist. The
intuition of free will; free will exercised for a purpose; purpose directed to clothe human life with

value; value measured by happiness—the chain is perfect, link by link, only at the end it seems to be attached to nothing. And so I ask myself, reluctantly, almost wishing my answer were mistaken, whether those who advocate humanism, as an isolated movement, are not doomed to disappointment. It is not that the direction in itself is wrong; every step in the program is right, and only by this path can we escape from the waste land of naturalism. But can we stop here in security? For purpose that will not end in bitter defeat; for values that will not mock us like empty masks, must we not look for a happiness based on something beyond the swaying tides of mortal success and failure? Will not the humanist, unless he adds to his creed the faith and the hope of religion, find himself at the last, despite his protests, dragged back into the camp of the naturalist? If we perish like beasts, shall we not live like beasts? I know that certain adherents of the present movement think they can avoid this fatality—notably Mr. Alan Reynolds Thompson, whose thesis, though concerned primarily with tragedy, may be extended to the whole range of literature:

. . . The dilemma of modern tragedy remains very real. There is no refuge in obscurantism through return to illusions which science has shattered. Reason denies the objective reality of our dreams; and so long as the honest man accepts a monism which identifies man with nature, he can find no justification for tragic exaltation. The humanist, however, denies the necessity for this identification. Without in the slightest degree disparaging the truth or worth of physical knowledge he maintains that the realm of value has significant validity when taken as distinct from the realm of fact. The realm of value belongs to man; that of fact, to outer nature.

Following this thesis, Mr. Thompson rejects the doctrine of poetic justice as formulated by Mr. Ludwig Lewisohn: "Serious drama deals with the transgressions of an immutable moral law by a self-originating will. . . . In each instance the destruction of the protagonist reconciles the spectator to a universe in which guilt is punished and justice is upheld." On the contrary Mr. Thompson declares that "the ethical victory of the tragic hero is not a vindication of a moral order in the universe"; rather, the exalted feeling we get from tragedy is due to our "admiration" of a hero "steadfast in his will even to death." That is to say, if I understand the argument: the realm of values connected with a moral order belongs to man not as a fact, but as a dream; and as human beings we must cling to this dream by a desperate act of admiration against the truth of reason which leaves to it no objective reality. Brave words, but so inhumanly difficult. I am troubled by the saying of Pascal that, unless man has the support of the supernatural, he will fall inevitably into Stoic pride or Epicurean relaxation. In our modern tongue that is equivalent to pronouncing that the humanist who thinks to stand without religion is desperately beset by forces that would sink him to the level of naturalism. He may cling stubbornly to values that are the creation of his own fancy—for a while; in the end he will be overcome by the brutality of facts.

Now humanism is concerned primarily with the manifestation of life in art and literature, and the question may thus arise as to the kind of religion, granted that some religion is necessary, which would serve as a sound basis for the exercise of the imagina-

tion. Well, I think one may say this at least without
hesitation, that it must be more than a vague acquiescence in a vaguer conception of something divine and
infinite floating far above the world in the vacuous
heaven of metaphysics, or oozing out of the world
like an opiate vapor to induce the reveries of pantheism. Nor can it be such a possession as may be
kept, so to speak, in a compartment by itself, as a
precious ornament to be contemplated in idle moments
and enjoyed in secret. It must be a militant force that
will intermeddle with the whole of life, exacting
obedience and arousing enmities. Nor, on the other
hand, can it, for the humanist at least, be such a
sublimation of the ethical will as would deprive this
transient world of significance and demand the total
renunciation of mortal ambitions and desires. On the
contrary it must come into the heart of man, not without austerity of command, yet with salutary hope,
assuring us that our practical sense of right and
wrong, of beauty and ugliness, is justified by the eternal canons of truth, and that the consequences of our
deeds in this little segment of space may follow the
soul in its flight into regions beyond our utmost
guessing. It must fortify the purpose of the individual
by inspiring him with a conviction that the world in
which he plays his part is not a product of chance or
determinism, but the work of a foreseeing intelligence, and is itself fulfilled with purpose. It must lend
new meaning and larger values to visible phenomena
by seeing in them shadows and symbols of invisible
realities, and by exhibiting them as servants to a spiritual end. It will so knit the future with the present,
so bind together the eternal and the temporal, that

the torment of frustration will be assuaged, the sting of transience blunted, and the triumph of the grave overthrown. Only so will happiness be possible here and now as at once the duty and the reward of man. Thus religion was understood by Socrates, in the great age of Grecian achievement, when he consoled his friends in the hour of his apparent defeat: "Wherefore be of good cheer about death, and know of a certainty that no evil can happen to a good man, either in life or after death; he and his are not neglected by the gods." Thus it was proclaimed by a greater than Socrates, again in the hour of apparent defeat, when he comforted his disciples with words that might be interpreted as a divine response to the Socratic faith: "Peace I leave with you, my peace I give unto you: not as the world giveth, give I unto you. In the world ye have tribulation; but be of good cheer, I have overcome the world."

It does not follow, if what I have said be true, that the art and literature of a creative era must be exclusively or even predominantly religious in intention, or that every individual artist must be a believer. But I think it would not be difficult to prove from history that wherever great art has flourished, noble in theme as well as in technique, there religion such as I have described it, though the ingredients may vary in proportion and degree and tone, has been present in the background, colouring the thoughts and emotions of society and investing the natural world with a glamour of the supernatural. On the other hand it is equally true that religion, even when favourable in spirit, does not automatically produce a humanistic age, while in some of its manifestations it has been actually antagonistic to art and humane letters. There is need also of a humanism, aroused to its own dignity and ardently concerned with the beautiful representation of life as well as with life itself.

CONTENTS OF *HUMANISM AND AMERICA*

NORMAN FOERSTER: *Preface.*

LOUIS TRENCHARD MORE: *The Pretensions of Science.*

IRVING BABBITT: *Humanism: An Essay at Definition.*

PAUL ELMER MORE: *The Humility of Common Sense.*

G. R. ELLIOTT: *The Pride of Modernity.*

T. S. ELIOT: *Religion Without Humanism.*

FRANK JEWETT MATHER, JR.: *The Plight of our Arts.*

ALAN REYNOLDS THOMPSON: *The Dilemma of Modern Tragedy.*

ROBERT SHAFER: *An American Tragedy.*

HARRY HAYDEN CLARK: *Pandora's Box in American Fiction.*

STANLEY P. CHASE: *Dionysus in Dismay.*

GORHAM B. MUNSON: *Our Critical Spokesmen.*

BERNARD BANDLER, II: *Behaviour and Continuity.*

SHERLOCK BRONSON GASS: *The Well of Discipline.*

RICHARD LINDLEY BROWN: *Courage and Education.*

IRVING BABBITT

[First published in the *University of Toronto Quarterly* for January 1934; later in the *American Review* for April 1934]

IT IS not an easy thing, with the cold page of print in mind, to write of a friend, a very close friend, and it is only with reluctance that I have acceded to the request to undertake such a task. And there was a special reason for hesitating in this case. Babbitt was an author and a teacher, and in these capacities is known to a larger and a smaller circle; others may estimate—indeed Professor Mercier has already estimated—the value of his books as well as I could do, or better; and of his astonishing manner and power in the lecture room, his pupils, many of them now holding prominent places in the academic world, can speak from a knowledge which I do not possess. But he was a talker too, greater in that vein, I believe, than as a teacher, greater, I know, than as an author. And it is just of his genius in the give and take of conversation that I am qualified, by long association and by a fundamental sympathy of mind not incompatible with clashing differences, to write as probably no one else can do. Yet a record of the spoken word without its intonation and the accompanying gesture leaves it but a dead thing, and a reported argument is likely to lose its point unless the second party to the discussion brings himself into the scene to a degree that may seem egotistic.

My acquaintance with Babbitt began in the autumn of 1892, when I came to Cambridge from the West to prosecute my study of Sanskrit and Pâli. Babbitt was then twenty-six or -seven years old. He had graduated from Harvard, had taught for a time in Montana, and had then spent a year in Paris, working in the same languages with Sylvain Lévi. We two formed the whole of the advanced class under Professor Lanman, and naturally were thrown much together. I can well remember our first meeting in Lanman's marvellously equipped library. Babbitt was rather above the average height, powerfully built, with the complexion of radiant health. But it was his eyes that caught and held one's attention. They were of a dark, not pure blue, and even then, though of a lustre that dimmed somewhat in later years, had in repose the withdrawn look of one much given to meditation. He had a way of gazing downwards or forwards or anywhere rather than into the face of his interlocutor, in a manner which could never be described as timid or shifty, but which gave often the impression of remoteness, as if he had lost the individual before him in some general view of life or some question of fundamental principles which might be occupying his mind. But if the unlucky individual thought to escape into that remoteness from the consequences of a rash statement or a logical fallacy, he was likely to be caught up by a swift direct glance that seemed to shoot out tentacles, as it were, into his very soul. At such moments that restless energy of Babbitt's, which was wont to work itself off in walking or by pacing back and forth as he talked, would appear to be gathered together, holding his body in an attitude of tense rigidity. The

effect—-I am speaking of his early years of combat—
was startling, sometimes almost terrific, as if in an
evening ramble under the shadow of familiar trees
one were brought up sharply by the gleam of watching
eyes from a form crouching ready to spring. One such
instance I may recall. We were strolling up what was
then known as North Avenue, engaged in debate over
I cannot remember what matter, when suddenly he
stopped short, faced about upon me, and, with both
hands rigidly clenched, ejaculated: "Good God, man,
are you a Jesuit in disguise?" The words may sound
flat enough in the repeating; but as they were hurled
out, with the accompanying gesture and glance of
indignation, they made an impression not to be forgotten. I have never been able to answer the question
satisfactorily.

The old North Avenue and Brattle Street, both
thoroughfares at that time leading out into the open
country, are particularly associated in my memory
with these talks. Babbitt was always delicately sensitive to the charms of New England scenery, and in
such places as Squam Lake and Dublin, N.H., where
later I visited him in the long vacations, he would
manifest a romantic love of nature which might sur-
prise those who know only the classical and rather
austere side of his intellect. But again, in those Cambridge days, owing to the weather or the hour we
would meet indoors, sometimes in his room, oftener
in my own narrow quarters. And I can see, almost
hear, him now as he used to pace back and forth the
few steps from wall to wall, arguing vehemently on
whatever question might be broached, or recounting
the adventures of his youth (a strange and mixed

experience), pausing at every fourth or fifth turn to take huge draughts from the water jug on my washstand, and pretty well emptying it in the course of an evening. I cannot recall the range of topics discussed—no doubt in part they were those which young men have been worrying over since the beginning of human speech—nor can I recapture the excitement of hearing the world and the destinies of man tossed about in thesis and counter-thesis after a fashion quite new to me. Literature was one of the fields in which he exercised his dialectic, naturally; and what remains with me now is chiefly the fact that his views were already formed and fixed. My taste, on the contrary, was in a state of transition. I had brought with me to Cambridge a mind steeped in Heine and Novalis and the Schlegels, and though my enthusiasm for these German dreamers had cooled before I met him and I was feeling my way towards more classical standards, there was enough of the old virus left in me to call out all the vigour of his critical powers. I am afraid that I held for him then the place afterwards occupied by Rousseau, who in those days, so far as I can remember, was never mentioned, but first comes to the front in the comparison with Bacon in *Literature and the American College,* one of Babbitt's best and most finished pieces of writing and an epitome of all he was to fight for in later years. Of the classics Horace, I think, was at that time the poet most frequently referred to or quoted by him. And at the frosty touch of that Lord of Common Sense the exquisites of romanticism would shrivel up and drift away in the winds. How he came to his love and mastery of the Roman and Greek poets, I do not know. According to his own account the taste was born in him. The astonishing fact, as I look back over the years, is that he seems to have sprung up, like Minerva, fully grown and fully armed. No doubt he made vast additions to his knowledge and acquired by practice a deadly dexterity in wielding it, but there is something almost inhuman in the immobility of his central ideas. He has been criticized for this and ridiculed for harping everlastingly on the same thoughts, as if he lacked the faculty of assimilation and growth. On the contrary, I am inclined to believe that the weight of his influence can be attributed in large measure to just this tenacity of mind. In a world visibly shifting from opinion to opinion and, as it were, rocking on its foundation, here was one who never changed or faltered in his grasp of principles, whose latest word can be set beside his earliest with no apology for inconsistency, who could always be depended on. It will be remembered that Socrates was charged with the same monotony of ideas, and his retort to the sophist might have been uttered by Babbitt: "Why, my dear young man, not only am I always talking in the same manner, but I am forever talking about the same things." It comes down to one's conception of truth: is truth something fixed which can be discovered, and when discovered is it of a nature to demand a man's unwavering allegiance; or is truth too, like opinion, only a glimpse of some momentary aspect of the flux, no sooner beheld than lost in the flowing stream of impressions?

And not only had Babbitt at an early age—how early I do not know—reached these settled convictions, but at least from the beginning of our acquaintance they were knit together into a system by logical bonds which were perfectly clear to his mind, so clear, indeed, that he tended to take them for granted as equally obvious to others. The consequence to his writing was not wholly fortunate. For one thing, it gave a kind of rotary movement instead of a regular progression to his books. A rhetorician would say that he did not know how to manage his paragraphs. Instead of finishing one link of his argument and then proceeding to the next and so on from premise to conclusion, he is somewhat inclined to crowd his whole thesis, at least implicitly, into each single paragraph, so that the book, despite the inexhaustible variety of his illustrations, gives the impression of endless repetition. That is undoubtedly a fault of construction, and has stood in the way of his full recognition as a thinker. But it is a rhetorical fault only, owing to a failure to put himself as a writer into the mind of his reader; the constructive faculty was really there; he had reasoned out his position step by step, but, having done this for himself, he would forget that his reader had not been present at the process, and he would pitch into his exposition at any point— beginning, middle, or ending.

And this is one reason why he seemed to me more effective as a talker than as a writer. Here again the uninstructed or uninterested listener might criticize his conversation as displaying the same lack of method as his books. And I can remember the complaint of a distinguished but rather commonplace historian of Harvard that my friend's conversation had no sense at all, being a jumble of terms with no definite meaning for him or for anyone else, and of dogmatic assertions which severally had no logical basis and collectively no sequence. But for the sympathetic listener there needed to be no such difficulty. By a question interposed here and there, or by an occasional sharp contradiction, it was easy to bring him back to the order of his thoughts and to lay bare the whole hidden working of his mind from axiomatic principles to inevitable conclusions.

I am trying to describe Babbitt's talk at its highest, when the subject brought out all his resources, and to show how, in the give and take of argument and by the need of defending his position against an antagonism not incompatible with large agreement, certain qualities came to the light which many readers fail to detect in his published works. But I would not leave the impression that he was addicted to preaching in season or out of season; there might be something of the prophet in his tone when grave moral issues were raised, never of the prig; he might reduce his antagonist physically to a rag by the pertinacity of his attack, he was never a bore. His ordinary intercourse, as a matter of fact, was notable for flashes of wit and strokes of keen repartee that could set the table on a roar, and in his earlier days might be seasoned by touches of almost Rabelaisian humour which would never be guessed from the reticences of his later manner.

Literature and the problems of education were much in his thought; but the staple of his more serious talk, owing chiefly to his own inclination but partly, no doubt, to provocation from my side, was ethical and religious. This remained true to the end; in those days, however, the discussions were coloured by his, or I may say our, special studies. From the beginning, Babbitt was drawn to the Buddhistic side of Hinduism rather than to the Brahmanic, and to the Pâli language, in which the most authentic record of Buddha's teaching is preserved, rather than to the Sanskrit. There was something in this corresponding to his classical taste in works of the imagination and to his rejection of romanticism. Primarily what attracted him to the Pâli texts may have been the clarity and concreteness of the style (which the uninitiated may best feel in De Lorenzo's Italian version of *I Discorsi di Buddho*), as compared with the elusive mistiness of the Sanskrit, particularly of the *Upanishads*. With this clarity, almost hardness, of expression went the ethical doctrine of Buddha. Here I am unable to say whether Babbitt favoured the doctrine, the *dhamma*, because it fell in with conclusions at which he had already arrived by independent reflection, or whether his ethical ideas were largely the result of reading in the Pâli. Of the two alternatives I surmise that the former is the truer, though in either case the important point is the native affinity of his mind with that of the Oriental sage. This comes out in a footnote to his criticism of the Arcadian dream of Rousseau in his first publication:

The greatest of vices according to Buddha is the lazy yielding to the impulses of temperament (*pamâda*); the greatest virtue (*appamâda*) is the opposite of this, the awakening from the sloth and lethargy of the senses, the constant exercise of the active will. The last words of the dying Buddha to his disciples were an exhortation to practise this virtue unremittingly.

That was the lesson Babbitt had for the world when I first knew him; it is the heart and essence of what he inculcated in book after book, to the discomfiture and disgust of his hostile critics; it is what he was hoping to confirm by a translation and exposition of the *Dhammapada* which he was preparing when his health failed.

On the other hand, I had started my Oriental studies with a predilection for the Sanskrit literature of the *Upanishads,* the *Bhagavad Gîta,* and the Vedantic theosophy. To this I was brought in part, I suppose, by the romantic virus not yet expelled from my system, though a deeper attraction was in the mythological elements of the Vedânta, which, in fact, range from an absolute pantheism to a grotesque polytheism, but which might lead, as I think I even then felt instinctively, to a more concrete monotheism. However that may be, it is easy to see that here was a situation to call out all Babbitt's fighting powers in debate; and nobly did he respond to the summons. I would never acknowledge defeat, but I was often left prostrate on the field of battle.

This Harvard period extended over three years, the first when we were students together, the second when he returned as instructor in French after an interval of a year at Williams, and the third in 1899-1900 when I was there again doing some special work for Lanman. It is a digression but a fact worthy of note that, though Babbitt began—and ended—his teaching career at Harvard in the modern field, his heart at first was set on working in the classics. I often wonder what might have been the consequences if the Classical Department had not rejected him at the beginning and continued systematically *more suo* to ignore him. What might have happened if he had spent his energies on expounding a literature to which he could have given his positive allegiance instead of one which he studied chiefly to annihilate? His diagnosis of our modern ailments would have lost something of its fervour and scientific completeness; but the exemplary wisdom of Greece might have been brought back to us alive, and the teaching of the classics might have been made once more a discipline in the humanities. I may be pardoned for adding here my complaint that a very great teacher, perhaps even the greatest this country has ever produced, was overlooked by one department and, where accepted, had to force his way up against resistance and through protracted depreciation. There was a moment in his mid-career when it was even touch and go whether he would not be dropped altogether. It was the response to his genius by a large and growing number of the better students in the University that ultimately brought full recognition from the Faculty. But this is a digression.

A long period elapsed before the discussions of that early association were renewed in all their intimacy and intensity. During this interval I had visited him more than once in his summer homes and he had passed a number of months in Princeton, but the real fun began again in the second term of the academic year 1925-1926 (if my dates are correct), when I was a substitute at Harvard for an absent member of the Classical Department. Fortunately I was able to rent the home of Professor Ropes, who also was enjoying a "sabbatical." There was a large and comfortably furnished library attached to the house, and here night after night, two or three times a week, Babbitt used to come, and, sitting on one side of the great fireplace, with me—shall I say, his glad victim?—on the

other side, poured out such a stream of argument,
invective, and persuasion as had not, I am sure, been
heard in Cambridge before and probably will never
be heard again. It was *magnifique, et c'était la guerre!*
The battle-ground was the same as in the old Harvard
days, but with a difference. Babbitt's fundamental
ideas had not changed by a jot, though they were now
reinforced by an appalling mass of erudition at the
service of an unhesitating, unfailing, unerring memory. Meanwhile, I had quite definitely moved away
from my absorption in the theosophical speculations
of India; my heart was now all in a Platonism supple-
mented by Christian theology of the Greek type.
Against the Platonic philosophy of Ideas, Babbitt
brought up Aristotle's positive and scientific humanism, and with the claims of theology contrasted the
merits of Buddha's non-theological religion which
offered the same ethical and spiritual results as Christianity without demanding credence in a dogma and
a mythology impossible, he insisted, for the modern
mind to accept. Of course my cue was to contend
that Aristotle himself, seeing that his positive humanism could not stand on its own feet, was driven at the
last to brace it with a metaphysic of the Absolute
beside which Plato's Idealism is as easy to swallow
as a breath of spring air, and that in religion Buddha
had won his army of adherents by the example of his
own supposed ascent through countless aeons to absolute knowledge, a myth as difficult to credit as the
Incarnation. Naturally I thought at the time I was
right, as I still think; but if victory ever lodged on my
side, it was of a very private sort, known only to

myself when I had crept to bed. But oh the wonder and glitter of those defeats!

It will be seen how Babbitt's attitude towards the great religions of the world might be brought out in such debates with a sharpness that would scarcely be guessed by those who know him only in his books. And this is particularly true in the case of Christianity, where for a double reason he exercised a certain reserve, or "economy," in his public statements. For one thing, he wrote always not for display but for conviction. His mind was eminently practical in that he aimed at getting results and thought much of strategy in attack. He held it a law of sound tactics not to arouse the hostility of those whom he desired to convince, but to make concessions where this could be done with honour; and he used to scold me laughingly, sometimes almost pathetically, for going out of my way, as he said, to make enemies among every party to a controversy. Thus it was that he took pains in his writing to avoid irritating the sensibility of Christian readers. But besides the strategic motive, perhaps explaining it, was the fact that he recognized in what he would call the psychological effects of dogmatic faith a moral and spiritual discipline to be acclaimed and fostered, whatever its source might be. He saw, and admitted wholeheartedly, that belief in the Grace of God had in times past operated to awaken the soul "from the sloth and lethargy of the senses," and to produce a "constant exercise of the active will" profoundly akin to the *appamâda* of Buddhism. In all this there was not the slightest intention to deceive or to palter about first principles; but it happened, nevertheless, that many Christians were misled by

these concessions. The dogma of Grace, the notion of
help and strength poured into the soul from a superhuman source, was in itself repugnant to him, and the
Church as an institution he held personally in deep dis-
taste, however he may have seemed to make an exception of the disciplinary authority of Romanism. There
should be no misunderstanding left on this point. The
naked truth will, I believe, redound to his credit; it
will clarify and strengthen his influence with the large
body of his pupils who feel the need of religion but
cannot subscribe to a definite creed. I can remember
him in the early days stopping before a church in
North Avenue, and, with a gesture of bitter contempt, exclaiming: "There is the enemy! there is the
thing I hate!" Undoubtedly that sentiment was softened as time went on, and as he grew more charitably
disposed towards those who, for whatever reason,
were ranged on the side of decency and restraint;
but it never disappeared. On the other hand, he was
much closer to Buddhism than would appear from his
public utterances. I wish not to exaggerate. In private
as well as in public he refused to be denominated a
Buddhist, and with perfect sincerity. But in the denial
by Buddha (the real Buddha as seen in the authentic
texts) of anything corresponding to Grace, in his
insistence on the complete moral responsibility of the
individual, in the majesty of his dying command,
"Work out your own salvation with diligence,"
Babbitt perceived the quintessential virtue of religion,
purged of ephemeral associations, of outworn superstition, of impossible dogma, of obscurantist faith,
and based on a positive law which can be verified by
experiment, pragmatically, step by step. It was in

this way he sought to bring together a positivism in the religious plane with a positivism in what he distinguished as the purely humanistic plane of life and letters.

So much I can say to elucidate what might be gathered from his books. And it seems to me worth saying for the reason that, however pungent and straightforward his language may be in other matters, his frequent allusions to the supernatural left a good many of his readers puzzled over its exact relation to the natural. The difficulty is that in print, so far as I remember, he never distinguishes between the supernatural and the superhuman, or makes clear why he accepted the one and rejected the other. Now Buddhism holds to the supernatural, holds to it, indeed, in the extreme form of an Absolute utterly different from, and separable from, the flux and disintegration and relativity of the natural. But the supernatural so conceived is, properly speaking, not superhuman; it is within man, a part of man's being, just as the natural is; and the ultimate goal of ethics and religion is a state wherein, entirely by human effort, the dualism in man of the supernatural and the natural is dissolved, and all the passions and insatiate desires and all the unattainable strivings of nature are forever stilled. In Christianity, on the other hand, the supernatural in man is regarded as akin to, but not identical with, a supernatural which is also superhuman. Grace is the medium of cooperation between the supernatural will in man and the divine will which is God.

With this distinction between the supernatural and the superhuman in mind one can understand how Christianity brings a disturbing factor into "humanism" as Babbitt conceived it, whereas Buddhism falls quite easily into the whole scheme. Humanism has to do primarily with that plane of practical ethics where the natural and the supernatural meet together, producing a world of harmony and order and mediation. Religion is an attempt to live in a plane above the humanistic, where the supernatural departs from the natural into its own citadel of imperturbable peace. Humanism is thus not anti-religious, in so far as it depends on the controlling power of the supernatural; but it may be non-religious in so far as its business is with the world and does not seek to escape the world. The humanist is not hostile to religion, but he should be careful not to confuse the plane of the non-religious with that of the religious. At the same time, his passage from the non-religious to the religious plane, when he wishes to make it, is simplified by the fact that the higher sphere is still human in the sense that no demand is made upon him to go outside of himself (his higher self), nor to introduce any element of the superhuman as contrasted with the supernatural which was already present and operative in the humanistic sphere.

All this I could understand from our conversations at Harvard. But there was still something in Babbitt's personal attitude towards religion not clear to me, and I had even ventured in an essay published in *The Bookman* to challenge him on this point. In response he said more than once that the time had come when he ought to define his position in such terms as to leave no room for misunderstanding; and this, in fact, he undertook to do in the Introduction to his essays *On Being Creative*, published in 1932. But even there

his definition is so complicated with his whole theory
of humanism that I doubt if it has cleared up all the
difficulties which his followers had felt; the weakness
of the written word, as Plato long ago complained, is
that it can make no reply to the questioner. And that
is why I would supplement his published *apologia*
with a reference to a last conversation with him not
many months before his health was finally broken.

It was at my home in Princeton. We were sitting in
a flagged porch looking out over a stretch of lawn to
a background of shrubs and trees arrayed in the rich
greens of early summer and bathed in the slanting
light of late afternoon. Something of the magic charm
of nature, to which Babbitt was always warmly responsive, perhaps also a foreboding of the end so near,
opened his heart, and he spoke of his religious convictions with a simplicity and gentleness quite different from his ordinary combative manner. It was like
a confession of faith, to be held sacred except in so
far as it may serve to complete and elucidate his
public profession.

There is in man as distinguished from the animal,
he said, a something of which he is immediately,
though it may be dimly, aware at the centre of his
being, a something which exists apart from the desires
and affections and ambitions and dejections of that
lower self which is ordinarily thought of as our personality. It may be called the "ethical" will, because,
though not to be confused with the lower will which
is active in the affairs of life, it does yet, in some
untraceable manner, make its effects felt ethically in
the plane of nature. To express this indefinable relation, while maintaining intact the distinction between

the supernatural and the natural, the higher faculty may be spoken of as the will to refrain, the *frein vital* as contrasted with the *élan vital;* but though it can be defined only in negative terms, it is in itself real and positive, the highest reality and the supreme factor in that which we know as our individual character. At the same time, in this deepest stratum of our consciousness, we are aware of the great paradox that this ethical will is at once both individual and universal, so that he who is most himself is also most human, thinking and acting not as an isolated atom in conflict with other atoms, but as a being at one with the great heart of the world, strong in the strength drawn from that silence of the soul beyond the curtain of perplexing lights and noises, wherein all distractions end in peace.

I should be untrue to myself if I did not say that the refusal to admit responsibility to the superhuman, in the full theistic sense of the word, seems to me to deprive religion of its richest source of inspiration, and to leave it too often a sort of flimsy and unpractical sentiment. But I should be false to my friend if, with that last conversation in mind, I did not assert that, beneath all the fret of controversy, he himself had reached to a fountain of perennial peace and strength. In his books he may have written sometimes vaguely, and not always consistently, of religion; his life was a steady growth, not in Grace, but in obedience to the unrelenting exactions of conscience and in a sense of the littleness of men protesting against the law of their own being. There lay at once his humility and his magnanimity, and therein shines the virtue of his example.

Some time ago I was dining with Frank Mather, whom Babbitt had first met at Williams, and who from that association had come to be united with us in bonds of triple comradeship. He, too, as all readers are aware, is an advocate of humanism, and contends that only the perfect agnostic can lay claim to the Simon-Pure article. Among the guests was a Hindu gentleman of broad culture and keen perceptions, who had been recently in Cambridge and through my introduction had called on Babbitt. In the course of the evening, I asked him how Babbitt had impressed him, and his response was quick and enthusiastic: "Oh, Babbitt, he is a holy man, a great saint!" Now holiness is the last trait that most of us in the West would attribute to one of Babbitt's self-assertive character, but the word came quite naturally from an Oriental to whom the saint is a man notable rather for his will-power than for meek submissiveness. It was, perhaps, because I ventured upon some criticism of this kind that the Hindu visitor put me in my place: "You are not a saint at all, but only a philosopher"; and then, answering a question of our host about himself, added, with a twinkle in his eye: "And you, my dear Frank, are the wickedest man I know."

PROUST: THE TWO WAYS

[Published in the *American Review* for April 1933]

THERE is something portentous in the life of Marcel Proust; something portentous in the vast work of fiction into which his life was poured; something equally portentous in the kind of homage given to that work by admirers, many of whom have read but a small portion of it. Of the life little need here be said. It may be assumed that every one interested in the subject knows how the young Parisian, born into a rich family of the bourgeoisie, became a pet of the fashionable circle of the old French nobility, how from childhood he was the victim of a neurotic affection which took the form of asthma, how in his later years he shut himself up in a chamber closed against all ventilation and lined with cork, and how in this artificial seclusion (broken until the very end by hysterical eruptions into society) he laboured with demonic energy to complete the long novel in which he should wreak his contempt of the world.

As for the novel itself, it is portentous in its mere length and portentous in its power of combining unity of purpose with dispersion of method.[1] The *Overture* to the first volume begins with a curious analysis of

[1] In the original, *A la Recherche du temps perdu* is divided into seven parts extending to sixteen volumes. My quotations are from the excellent translation of C. K. Scott Moncrieff who completed all but the last of the ten volumes of the English version.

sleep and waking, and their merging together in the
dream-state, which is meant to set the tone for all
that follows. Through the power of memory we then
have an evocation of the life of the hero (called
Marcel, and in fact a shadowy image of the author
himself) as a child in the home of his great-aunt at
Combray, where three generations of the family are
gathered. We hear about the vagaries of an aunt,
Léonie, who is a hypochondriac confined to her room,
about the boy's passionate love for his mother (not
without hints of Freudian "complex"), about the
visit of a wealthy Jewish connoisseur of the arts
named Swann. But the happenings, slight enough in
themselves, are bathed in a flood of fancies and reflections, "shifting and confused gusts of memory,"
started by the chance perception of some flower or bit
of water or church spire, or by some trivial event such
as the taking of a crumb of cake or a spoonful of tea.
In the main these impressions are connected with
walking or driving excursions along two roads, one
of which passes the country seat of the Guermantes',
a family which traces its various ramifications back
to the heroic names of antiquity, while the other leads
to Méséglise past the homes of Swann and of the
musician Vinteuil. It is at Montjouvain, a place on
this second way, that an adventure occurs to "Marcel" (we know that something similar had happened
to the real Marcel) which is to haunt him through life
and is to form the pattern, so to speak, for his pictures
of society. To put it briefly, he sees through an open
window the daughter of Vinteuil engaged with a girl
friend in a passionate display of anomalous love (I

prefer this less repulsive phrase for homosexuality) intensified by sadism.

To my taste this introductory section, including the *Overture* and *Combray,* is the subtlest and truest and most interesting portion of the whole novel. It is highly original, often quaint and exquisite, and it is adroit as a preparation for what follows; best of all, it is comparatively short.

For the rest the substance of the novel, so far as it has any, is the doings of the people of the two ways, the aristocratic circle of the Guermantes Way and the bourgeois circle of Swann's Way, told not in the ordinary style of narration but in interminably protracted accounts of dinners and receptions at this or that house, ending with an assembly at the Princesse de Guermantes's, in *The Past Recaptured,* where we see the old standards of snobbishness broken down and the two streams of society mingled together in a débâcle of all standards whatsoever. And what society! I once at a dinner heard Mr. W. B. Yeats explaining the difference between the group of poets to which he belonged when he first came up to London and the group which now disports itself there. "We," said he, with a twinkle in his eye, "had the manners of bishops and the morals of brigands; our successors have the manners of brigands and the morals of bishops." For the manners and morals of M. Proust's society you may leave out the bishops. If the record is meant to be satire, it is too improbable to sting; if it is meant to be fun, it is too ill-natured (and too monotonous) to amuse. Much of it is well skipped.

The nearest approach to a full-length portrait is the grotesque figure of the Baron de Charlus (a Guermantes), ravaged and in the end pitifully broken by his anomalous passions. The nearest approaches to *consecutive* narration are the story of Swann's wooing of Odette and the story of Marcel's love for Albertine. But in neither of these two stories are there any events such as make the staple of the ordinary novel. Swann's experience resolves into the fluctuating emotions of a man who is consciously making a fool of himself, and Marcel's love, when it once gets started, scarcely moves out of a flux and reflux of jealous suspicions that extend through seven hundred and fifty-seven pages. And the portrait as well as the stories are simply drowned in a billowing ocean of reflections on every aspect of life. It is in fact this stream of ideas, chiefly psychological, led on and on by an unpredictable association, this, rather than the sporadic events, that forms the matter of the book; and our critical estimation of Proust will depend largely on our judgement of the soundness or unsoundness of his psychology. For myself I may say that I find these reflections in part surprisingly fine and fresh, in part tediously commonplace, in part vitiated by a fundamentally inadequate conception of human nature, in part sheer nonsense. The amazing thing is that any writer could keep up the process so continuously and so long. When all is said, it is a prodigy of the creative will and intellect; and I suspect that many readers' wonder at the immensity of the achievement passes into admiration for its quality. Held in a kind of breathless suspense at the spectacle, as at the sight of a man walking a tightrope over the whirlpool of Niagara, they forget to ask themselves whether the performance is anything more than a prodigious waste of skill and endurance. What, we may well ask, does all this display of cleverness amount to, after all? To what common end have the two ways, so carefully described at the beginning, brought us?

The fact is that, however Proust may distinguish between the two ways of society, of the two ways open to the creative imagination he knows but one, and has pursued it with a persistence and sagacity and intrepidity which have earned for him something like prophetic repute among those of his generation who are treading with less certainty the same road to the same goal. It is not a wide renown, or, if wide, is a renown largely of mystification. To the generality of men, bound over to a succession of little unending tasks, and content in the respites of toil to snatch at any diversion of pleasure or to sit in somnolent expectation—to these the world of Proust, if known at all, must be a pure bewilderment, and the drift of his moral psychology must be like the shimmering of gossamer filaments blown from their attachment.

> For most men in a brazen prison live,
> Where, in the sun's hot eye,
> With heads bent o'er their toil, they languidly
> Their lives to some unmeaning taskwork give,
> Dreaming of nought beyond their prison-wall.

But there are some, a growing number today, who, in their minds at least, have broken away from the treadmill of business, and are asking what it all means and why it should be. To most of these the old answers are no longer valid; tradition seems indeed to be the mere negation of liberty and the very warden of the brazen walls they would escape.

And the rest, a few,
Escape their prison, and depart
O'er the wide ocean of life anew.
There the freed prisoner, where'er his heart
Listeth, will sail.
Nor doth he know how there prevail,
Despotic on that sea,
Trade-winds which cross it from eternity.

These, I take it, the rebels determined to be free, yet a little dubious of their goal, form the band of Proust's votaries. It is the imagination that sets them at large, and to the imagination they look for a pilot over the uncharted seas. Alert and curious, they are ready to acclaim the voice of any prophet who, like the Apostles of old miraculously delivered from gaol, comes to them accredited to speak "all the words of this life."

It is perhaps a truth not fully recognized that fear is one of the emotions attendant upon the liberty of thinking—just plain fear, running the gamut from intermittent moments of disquietude to an ever-present haunting horror. We begin to reflect, and forthwith our thought acts as a kind of dissolvent upon the solid-seeming fabric of life. The successive tasks in which we are engaged, the sequence of events through which we pass, cease to be separate tenable facts, rising out of the tides of time like isolated rocks, and melt into fluid fluctuant forms like the waves that toss about them. We appear to be adrift on a waste expanse of racing shadows; the only certainty left us is the principle of uncertainty, and the only permanent thing discoverable is the law of impermanence. And with this dissolution of facts into the mist of unreality comes a corresponding disintegration of values. What significance can be given to these transient apparitions that constitute the world in which we live? What importance can be attached to the stream of sensations that make up our conscious existence? It may be that with the ordinary man these doubts are no more than faint and rarely recurrent impressions; but their possibility, their potentiality so to speak, is forever in the background, and as reflection deepens they may be consolidated into a state of abiding apprehension. "All things are in flux," cries Marcus Aurelius, "thou thyself art undergoing a perpetual transformation and, in some sort, decay, as is the whole universe." And day by day the frightened ruler of the world made time to write out the meditations in which he sought to solace himself for the depredations of change. His piety was strong enough to hold his imagination in check and to prevent it from conjuring up pictures of pure terror; but with others it is as if the web of circumstance floated before them like a thin vapour through the rifts of which their gaze plunged into a dizzy vertigo of nothingness. You have a Pascal terrified by the silence of the infinite spaces above and averting his eyes from the gulf ever yawning at his side. Or you have an Amiel, who could scarcely breathe for the sense of being suspended by a thread over the unfathomable abysses of destiny—in a kind of tête-à-tête, as he says, with the Infinite, which is only another name for the Great Death. You may disregard a Pascal and an Amiel as morbid visionaries, and indeed to a mind like Voltaire's one of them was a maniac; but in truth they differ from the rest of us only by the depth of their insight and the power of their imagination.

From that horror of emptiness there are various modes of escape. Philosophy has a way, pursued by the Stoics of old and their modern congeners. This film of visible phenomena, it declares, is like a curtain forward and backward rolled in everlasting recurrence; and beyond it lies nothing conceivable, not even the void; there is no beyond. What has been seen before is seen now, and what is seen now, shall be seen again. Where nothing could be imagined otherwise, there can be nothing amiss; and where nothing is amiss, there can be no reason for fear. It is not a joyous road, this of philosophy, but to the disciplined will it offers the grey-hued calm of acquiescence in the fact. And there is the way of religion, which avers that through and beyond the veil it discovers not emptiness but eternal realities of the spirit; and this path promises to lead to the peace of great joy.

But our present concern, except indirectly, is not with philosophy or religion, but with art, and more particularly with the art of fiction. And since, whether for good or for ill, the theme of the novel from the beginning has been predominantly love, we are to see in what different ways the imagination lays hold of this theme in its search for a world of reality.

Now it must be observed that what we call love is a highly complicated phenomenon. It has at the core a solid fact, the universal pressure of sex; but all about that natural impulse, enveloping and penetrating it, extends a network of sentiments and associations, epiphenomena so to speak, which are the potent factors in changing indiscriminate lust into what is properly called love. By sentiment I mean primarily that intensified craving for beauty which, with the ordinary man, especially perhaps in youth, comes suddenly with the incursion of desire. All men in love we say are potential poets. And, further, I mean that more unified sense of beauty, appearing now as loveliness, which arises as attention is centred upon a single person, producing often a curious complication of physical craving with a reticence of respect and crossing self-will with self-abnegation. As Professor Taylor observes in one of the fine passages of his *The Faith of a Moralist*: "When, in the dawn of adolescence, the 'young man's fancy lightly turns to thoughts of love,' he must be a very poor kind of young man if, from the very first, the promptings of mere animal 'passion' are not so overlaid with characteristically human affection and imagination that they are, for the most part, only in the background of consciousness."

Of the existence of this sentimental overlaying there can be no doubt. In one stage or another, to one degree or another, it is common to all men; but in its immediate form it is also more or less transient, unless reinforced by associations of another order, ethical rather than sentimental in the sense that the imaginatively heightened relation of two individuals, one to the other, is absorbed into the broader relations upon which rests the very structure of human society. After all, the normal outcome of physical union is offspring, and with children comes the family, and upon the family is built the intricate organization of the State.

All this is a commonplace, as it is equally a commonplace that physical desire and the sentiment of love and the recognition of social obligations in love do not necessarily coincide, or may coincide in various patterns. But it needs some reflection, perhaps, to see just how the two ways of fiction are defined by the attitude of the writer towards this complicated phenomenon, according as he looks for the significant reality in its core of physical urgency or in its envelope of sentimental and ethical associations. On the one way the novelist, while not denying, or even minimizing, the basic fact of sex, tends to keep it in the background as in itself an unmalleable force, common to men and animals and unimportant in the differentiation of man from man. What rather interests him is the sense of beauty that arises out of the brute fact as a flower springs from the earth, and that flourishes only with a certain reticence as to its source, just as the flower must not carry the soil on its blossom. But that is only the beginning of the divergence. The final parting of the ways comes with recognition of the ethical associations attached to love. Though he may not deal openly with the matter as would a professed moralist, though indeed as an artist he is bound more or less to deal with it indirectly, nevertheless the family and the structure of society are for him the important fact, the more important as his art rises in seriousness; and the personal sentiment of love in his imaginative world acquires dignity just in proportion as it can be carried on into this ethical sphere. The significant reality for him lies here for the reason that these associations have a validity above the happiness of the individual, being fixed by eternal principles of right and wrong interwoven into the very texture of human life. The people of his imagination may not know these laws, or, knowing, may disregard them;

but he knows. One of the readier sources of poignant
emotion at the disposal of the novelist is the breaking
of his fictitious persons, through their ignorance or
rebellion, against this wall of impersonal facts; but
the emotion will rise to the height of true tragedy
only when the manipulator of the puppets is himself
neither ignorant nor rebellious.

An impressive illustration of this artistic canon
may be seen in Richardson's *Clarissa,* the first full-
blooded novel ever written, and the fashioner of innumerable books to follow—first, that is, if we
disregard *Pamela* as a sort of preliminary sketch and
with it Fielding's roistering parody. The theme of
Richardson's tale is love and nothing but love, and
the whole plot might be summarized in the couplet:

> Much ado there was, God wot;
> He would love and she would not.

In one respect the hero and the heroine are in accord;
they each feel towards the other the primal impulse
of desire, and Clarissa, however discreetly the author
may deal with the subject, would have been quite
ready to throw herself into the arms of her wooer—
on a condition. That condition is marriage. Now marriage does not alter the physical fact in the least; and
so on its face the ceremony may appear to be no more
than the utterance of a few conventional words. But
it may also be regarded as the symbol and pledge
of something vastly significant added to the physical
fact. To Clarissa, though she might not have been able
to give an articulate account of her feelings, it meant
public recognition of the truth that the drawing of the
individual man to the individual woman should be
made subordinate to the circle of moral obligations

which are so nobly expressed in the old Roman
Statutes by the *consortium totius vitae,* and which had
for her the sanctity of a law divine as well as human.
Any attempt to free the physical fact from these conditions was fraught for her with horror. It is for this
reason that the success of Lovelace, carried through
with treachery and force, does not affect the reader
as brutal realism but rises into the plane of high tragedy. By some miracle of genius Richardson adapted
to the narrowest usage of fiction the ancient and never
concluded battle of *physis* (nature) and *nomos* (law),
which had once been waged so dramatically between
Socrates and the Sophists, as we read in the *Gorgias*
of Plato. And if with most of the successors of Richardson, beginning with his satirist, Fielding, marriage
and not rape is the *dénouement* of the plot, this only
means that a happy rather than a tragic ending is the
easier and, in general, the more normal treatment of
love in the medium of prose.

But suppose on the other hand the novelist, and
with him probably his circle of readers, has lost the
sense of ethical reality and in the social laws sees only
a traditional convention (*nomos,* as the sophists understood it) hampering and abridging the fulfilment of
individual desires (*physis*) to no purpose. He may or
may not retain feeling for the sentimental penumbra
about the physical fact. Without that feeling he will
write as a realist after the fashion of Zola, and his
interpretation of life, in so far as it adheres to love as
the main theme of the novel, will be of the type of
Nana. In the other case, the sentiment retained, but
detached from its moorings in the higher law (*nomos,*

as Socrates understood it), will float off into a sort of "symbolism." In this case the imagination becomes only a servant of the flesh, or will further evaporate into the so-called "stream of consciousness," after the manner of Proust, in which thought succeeds thought, and image follows upon image, under no other guidance than the haphazard "association of ideas" revived so unexpectedly from an older discredited psychology. But in either case—and this is a point that should not be obscured by a trick of terminology —the writer, whether realist or symbolist, will belong to the broader school of naturalism, in so far as he eliminates that faculty of responsible selection in the field of consciousness which, for the humanist, belongs to man only along with the "nature" common to man and the rest of the animal kingdom. And further it should be noted that both branches of the naturalistic school are alike in this, that they rob human activity of any purpose or ultimate meaning. The only difference is that with the realist the result is likely to be a kind of sullen despair or fierce hatred, showing itself in a deliberate recourse to the ugly and bestial as the ultimate truth of things, and producing a curious but bastard imitation of genuine tragedy, whereas with the symbolist the illusion and utter futility of life will reproduce itself in an art ever more and more fantastically unreal.

Certainly illusion, with its attendant train of desolate awakenings, is the underground of Proust's sentimental and naturalistic picture of life, as all his readers will admit, his admirers as readily as his detractors. The matter is admirably summed up at the conclusion of Léon Pierre-Quint's unmitigated eulogy:

The reader who traverses the Proustian universe, over-peopled with characters, is overwhelmed by the impression of a continuous desolation. In the author's company we pass through the drawing-rooms, through Sodom, Gomorrah, Venus.—One after another we are confronted with the vanity of love, the vanity of social activity, the anguish of desire, and, on the margins of madness, the passions which haunt the degraded as much as the superior, which throw their lives out of balance and overshadow all their pleasures. And in every class of society each single individual is the slave of the same illusions and set on the edge of the same abyss. Death brings no hope. The search for self-centred pleasure is the great and general law. But pleasure does not exist, and its pursuit is as vain as the zeal of the occultists to find the esoteric traditions, the philosopher's stone, the formula of happiness. . . . The word *nothingness* recurs over and over again in the books of Marcel Proust, like a warning signal.

In other words the reader of these books has come, like Dante in his infernal journey, to the brink of the dolorous Valley, so obscure and profound and nebulous that gazing downwards the eye discovers no resting place; he has reached the limbo of nature where the inhabitants, cut off even from the realism of hell, know only this:

Che senza speme vivemo in disio.

Let there be no mistake about this. M. Pierre-Quint is right. Humanity as portrayed in Proust's imagination is without aim, without joy, without peace, without outlook of any sort; his people have no occupation save to think about themselves, and in *le néant* beyond the phantasmagoria of unsatisfied and forever insatiable desires the only reality for them is the grinning figure of Fear. The author himself knew the malignity of that face; and the look of it gradually paralysed all power of normal association. His last days alternated between a feverish repulsion of society and a no less panic craving for companionship. Before his death even his own brother, a physician, was barred from his room, and was met with frightful violence on forcing a way in.

Nevertheless—and this is one of the paradoxes of modern taste—a growing circle of enthusiasts, mostly very young, pretend to read such works with avidity and suck some kind of pride out of the pretension. Why, one asks. And the answer, if one may believe them, is definite enough: their delight is not in the thing represented—and indeed life itself, they say, in any veracious account can give joy to no one—but rather in the act itself of representing. That is, they delight in Proust's art as something utterly detached from life, and as producing a reality of its own. At least M. Pierre-Quint is quite clear about this. As a mere imitation of life, he admits, the work of Proust affords no relief in the promise of a future existence, nor does it even offer the expectation, "like all the atheists from Lucretius to the scientists, that to the evolutionary process of the universe there corresponds a 'Progress of Humanity' "—which yet would be a sad comfort to the individual who is never to see the fruits of such Progress. Nevertheless there is hope here for him who will take it, a joy in the liberating function of art as a power that may lift the reader into a something real just because unrelated to life. "In the void, the nothingness, of [Proust's] universe, art is the basis of morality, as well as being the immediate of metaphysics"—a morality unconcerned with any responsibilities and a metaphysics unhampered by any actuality. And so M. Pierre-Quint quotes a sentence of Bergson which, as he says, might have been written by Proust (who was in fact steeped in the Bergsonian philosophy) : "Art has no other object than to set aside the symbols of practical utility, the generalities that are conventionally and socially accepted, everything in fact which masks reality from us, in order to set us face to face with reality itself." Thus we learn that "the true Proustian joy is a kind of beatitude, . . . the absolute of the artist's joy."

In all which, it must be admitted, our critic is doing no more than develop the claims made by Proust himself. In the long account of one of the assemblies at the Verdurins', for instance, the reflections aroused by the playing of Vinteuil's sextet in the mind of Marcel (hero of the novel at once, it is to be remembered, and shadowy duplicate of the novelist) run on similar lines. "If art," he asks, "was indeed but a prolongation of life, was it worth while to sacrifice anything to it, was it not as unreal as life itself?" No, here was something utterly severed from "the nullity that [he] had found in all [his] pleasures and in love itself"; here within his grasp was the true "superterrestrial joy, . . . an ineffable joy which seemed to come from Paradise."

Now all this, if taken quite literally, is nonsense. The simple truth, which ought to be known to any adult mind, is that pure art, art completely severed from actuality, just does not exist. Art may interpret, and so in a fashion re-create; it cannot create *ex nihilo*. This chatter about receiving the ineffable joys of Paradise from a reality unattached to anything real is the watery moonshine of an outworn romanticism. If there is pleasure to be derived from Proust—a pleasure beyond that in the mere adroitness of imitation—it is because his novel is a criticism of life as didactic as any that Matthew Arnold would demand, though a criticism pointing in a very different direction. And it may be added that Proust himself knew this perfectly well.

The magic of Vinteuil's sextet is in fact very much a prolongation of life, as Proust carefully informs us, and its spell is inseparable from enchantments out of the past. As Marcel listens, there comes back to him slowly, like a vast bulk gradually looming up through clouds of mist, that fatal scene at Montjouvain. It was the Lesbian companion of Mlle Vinteuil who had made the execution of the piece possible by disentangling, "from papers more illegible than strips of papyrus, dotted with a cuneiform script, the formula eternally true, forever fertile, of this unknown joy, the mystic hope of the crimson Angel of dawn" (*mon Dieu, quel galimatias!*); and the fineness of spirit which had enabled her to accomplish this was born of the "profound union between genius (talent, too, and even virtue) and the sheath of vices." The remoter cause of this glorious art was anomalous love and sadism; its effect, the "beatitude," "the ineffable joy of Paradise," was to remind Marcel that his mistress also had been an associate of Mlle Vinteuil's friend, and to plunge him back again into the torments of his impotent sickly jealousy.

We are entitled to ask the meaning of this paradoxical position of a writer who boasts of his art as in no sense a prolongation of life and in the same breath shows it to be rooted in one of the most concrete of animal passions. First of all we are justified, I think,

in taking it as confirmation of the view that the ways
of the symbolist and the realist in fiction are merely
accidental diversions on the main road of naturalism.
But for an explanation of the peculiar straddling
achieved by Proust we are pointed back to that horror
of the void which confronts the self-liberated soul.
As a symbolist he sees the solid fabric of life constantly dissolving into sentiment; and sentiment for
him is only another name for the stream of sensations
floating up from some dark centre of the subconscious
under the sway of accidental associations, ungoverned
by the will, controlled by no faculty of selection, never
solidifying into action. One thing within this field
of sentiment might seem to lend order to these
chaotic sequences, imposing upon them a semblance
of static calm by linking the sensation that has been
with the ever newly arising sensation—memory. A
good deal has been written about Proust's philosophy
of memory, which in the main he borrowed from
Bergson; and the very titles of his work as a whole,
A la Recherche du temps perdu, and of the last section of it in particular, *Le Temps retrouvé,* show how
seriously he himself took this element of sentimental
experience. Undoubtedly also one of the striking features of his art is the skill, amounting to genius, with
which he describes the chain of recollections evoked
by some trivial event or sudden observation. But in
the end memory, too, becomes a factor of despair; it
cannot re-create what is gone, or give present reality
to what was unreal in the past, or counteract the corrosions of time.

There is a long passage of thirty-odd pages in the
first part of *Cities of the Plain* that touches the quick

of the matter. Marcel is suffering from physical collapse, and in a state of cardiac exhaustion stoops down to take off his boots. And in the very act suddenly his bosom swells, he is filled with an unknown, divine presence; so that he shakes with sobs, and tears stream from his eyes. It is all a little absurd, and thoroughly neurotic; but for the patient very significant. The image that comes thus to his rescue is the recollected face of his grandmother—the only person in the whole story, it may be said, for whom he has a quite normal affection. So by the power of memory the being that he was as child and youth under her benign influence, the being that might have gained itself by losing itself in another, seems to be recaptured. He vows to cling to this sentiment as to a plank caught in a boundless sea of waves—and then follows the deadly destruction of analysis. What is memory? It resolves into strange incompatible impressions of survival and obliteration, an agonizing synthesis of resuscitation and annihilation, an incomprehensible contradiction of possession and loss, a "crown of thorns." At the last memory acts as a solvent that merges our waking into our sleeping state; it offers a dream cloud and nothing solid upon which the imagination can lay hold: "There is no great difference between the memory of a dream and the memory of a reality."

This vaunted philosophy of memory is no more than a "recoil in horror" from what Proust elsewhere calls the "fragmentary and gradual death that interpolates itself throughout the whole course of our life," our reliance upon it only a part of the futile "plaint of those most humble elements of the personality which are about to disappear," forever swallowed up

in the vast backward and abysm of time. It is all vain.
The great fear remains. The symbolist's hope of dis-
pelling illusion by a thinner illusion, or of attaining
solidity by rolling vapour upon vapour, is itself an
illusion of adolescence, a fantastic dream like Ixion's
of embracing heaven in a cloud, from which the
awakening is into a hell of self-pursuing torture:

Volvitur Ixion et se sequiturque fugitque.

The life of Proust himself, the lives of the romantics
through the past century, are evidence.

The whole content of Marcel's memory is coloured,
as we know, by that early scene at Montjouvain;
and this is indicative of the way in which Proust
mingles realism with symbolism in his treatment of
the fundamental—certainly at least for him fundamental—theme of fiction. Debarred by his naturalistic
limitations from finding anything real in the ethical
sanctions of love he is driven in his search for reality
down through the superimposed layers of sentiment
to the basic fact of animal desire. And we can follow
the descent step by step. He cannot stop with that
attraction between a man and any chosen woman,
which is the simplest form of the passion we call
"love," since this enhancement of the individual
object desired is the illusory work of the imagination.
As he says: "This love of ours, in so far as it is love
for one particular creature, is not perhaps a very real
thing." He cannot stop with the more promiscuous
desire of man for woman, since there is still in this
instinctive emotion a tendency to hamper itself with
the unreal conventions of society. And so he reaches
down to the lust of the invert as coming nearest to the

fact of pure physical pleasure uncontaminated by sentiment.

Proust's attitude towards this topic is curious and, it must be admitted, not consistent. On the one hand it evidently arouses in him an instinctive feeling of indignation, connected with a residue of traditional morality from which he has not entirely liberated himself. It is even here and there castigated as a vice— whatever a vice may be to a professed amoralist—and he has not reached the stage of frank justification held by a Gide. He often speaks of it as a left-over from an outworn civilization, and as a curse by which a few abnormal persons are plagued. The most successful portrait in all his gallery is the Baron de Charlus, in whom the slow disintegration of character under the sway of this passion has elements of true tragedy. But on the other hand it is represented as permeating society from top to bottom. Regularly when the normal attraction between man and woman is treated, the suspicion of a secret practice of this other passion by one party or the other creeps in to create jealousy if not open rupture. Practically the whole of *The Captive* and a large part of *The Sweet Cheat Gone,* as we have said, are devoted to the doubts of Marcel over his mistress Albertine and his attempts to discover whether she had been associated with the debauches of Mlle Vinteuil and her friend. Even Albertine's death does not put an end to the self-commiserations of the distracted lover; and indeed this whole section of the novel is one of the most astounding and, I must think, one of the most maudlin exhibitions of futility ever made in literature.

It is perhaps the ambiguity attached to homosexuality as at once "natural" and "unnatural" that drives the naturalist in Proust a step lower in his search for the ultimate fact. For there is yet another instinct which not only isolates anomalous desire from any sentimental waste in moral obligations, but concentrates the individual upon himself by the sadistic doubling of lust with cruelty, and wrings out the last possibility of physical sensation in the masochistic union of pleasure with pain. So we reach the rock bottom of "nature," the end of the way which is not that of the humanist. The starting point for Proust's interpretation of life was the scene at Montjouvain. The conclusion is the *Temple de l'Impudeur* maintained in Paris during the War by "the heir of so many great lords, princes of the blood or dukes," where Marcel spies upon him, now a pitiable old man, blind and paralysed, yet still to his creator a "Saint"— spies upon him chained to an iron bed and submitting to the tortures of the lash, and then. . . . So it was that M. de Charlus clung to *l'illusion de la réalité*.

Between the realistic brutality of Montjouvain and the Temple lies the vast expanse of Proust's symbolism. There is a curious naïveté in the enthusiasm of the freed prisoner who would set out upon that expanse, rejoicing in the prospect of sailing where he listeth:

> Nor doth he know how there prevail,
> Despotic on that sea,
> Trade-winds which cross it from eternity.

To be honest with him, I think that he really does know, and his joy is a pretence to mask the great fear.

As for the other than the Proustian way which we have tracked to the bitter end, I cannot clinch what I have been trying to say better than by closing with a few words on Mr. Edmund Wilson's study of our author in *Axel's Castle*. For a clear summary of the tortuous substance of the ten or (in the French, sixteen) volumes we are considering, the essay is all that could be desired. There is a sort of finality in Mr. Wilson's setting of the Proustian symbolism at that particular point in its progress towards "the systematic nonsense called Dadaism," where "the metaphysic implicit" in this form of art unites consciously with the explicit metaphysic of relativism.

For modern physics, all our observations of what goes on in the universe are relative: they depend upon where we are standing when we make them, how fast and in what direction we are moving—and for the Symbolist, all that is perceived in any moment of human experience is relative to the person who perceives it, and to the surroundings, the moment, the mood. The world becomes thus for both fourth dimensional—with Time as the fourth dimension. . . . And, as in the universe of Whitehead, the "events," which may be taken arbitrarily as infinitely small or infinitely comprehensive, make up an organic structure, in which all are interdependent, each involving every other and the whole; so Proust's book is a gigantic dense mesh of complicated relations: cross-references between different groups of characters and a multiplication of metaphors and similes connecting the phenomena of infinitely varied fields—biological, zoological, physical, aesthetic, social, political, and financial.

That is excellently well put, and it may be confirmed by Proust's own statement, in *The Past Recaptured,* of his theory of art as an attempt to stay the relativism of Time in the static present of Memory. It does something also to explain why so tedious a work (certainly tedious as a whole) is taken excitedly as a sort of gospel for the day by those minds which are bounded by the circle of modernism. And Mr.

Wilson is equally clear in his perception of the outcome of such a philosophy. "We begin to be willing,"
he says, "to agree with Ortega y Gasset that Proust
is guilty of the medieval sin of *accidia,* that combination of slothfulness and gloom which Dante represented as an eternal submergence in mud. For *A la
Recherche du temps perdu,* in spite of all its humour
and beauty, is one of the gloomiest books ever written." Nor is there any doubt in Mr. Wilson's mind as
to what underlies this gloom. "We begin," he continues, "to feel less the pathos of the characters than
the author's appetite for making them miserable.
[There is in fact no real pathos in Proust.] And we
realize that the atrocious cruelty which dominates
Proust's world, in the behaviour of the people in the
social scenes no less than in the relations of the lovers,
is the hysterical sadistic complement to the hero's
hysterical masochistic passivity. What, we ask, is the
matter with Proust?"

What indeed is the matter with Proust? It is not,
Mr. Wilson assures us, his lack of insight into the
moral issues of life. He is a great moralist and has in
this respect much in common with George Eliot.
(This, be it observed, of an author who derives the
moral fineness of his most human character, Robert
de Saint Loup, from his servitude to a wretched pros-
titute—as George Eliot would have done!) The fault
is not any weakness of the imagination or intellect,
for "imaginatively and intellectually Proust is prodig-
iously strong." It is rather that he represents the
furthest outpost of the symbolistic movement as a
reaction against nineteenth century naturalism, and
that nothing further can be expected of this literature

which has undertaken to build up a "world of the
private imagination in isolation from the life of society"; art for art's sake has brought us to the great
vacuum. Back to the "life of society" literature must
come, or perish of inanity. And what the life of
society means to Mr. Wilson we know from an
article of his in *The New Republic* for January 14,
1931, which is in fact a kind of epilogue to *Axel's
Castle*. Our whole industrial organization has broken
down, he declares, and the only escape from a complete *débâcle* is in Marxian communism of the Russian stamp or in something still more audacious.

So a sympathetic reader of Proust would escape the
horror of the void which lies at the end of the Proustian philosophy of symbolism. But is there no other
way?

I would maintain, in the first place, that Mr. Wilson
is wrong in describing symbolism as a revolt from
nineteenth century naturalism. It is a revolt from the
realistic way of naturalism merely to another way of
the same broad movement. And this explains why the
revolt, unable to create any reality of its own, and
unable to escape the narrow bounds that circumscribe
both ways, turns back in the end to the grossest realism. These airy imaginings of metaphor and simile
are really no more than vapours floating up from the
abyss of the subconscious where nature lies embedded
in the double slime of hysterical sadism and hysterical
masochism. The vapours melt away in the infinite
void, and we have left only "nature."

And I think Mr. Wilson only plunges more deeply
into the vicious circle when he proclaims a way of
escape by his later exchange of the individualistic

naturalism of Proust for the communistic naturalism of Marx. If there is any healing for our sickness it is by taking another way, which is unknown to the "symbolist" and holds to a reality quite different from that of the realist. Its rejection of the Marxian gospel of economics is not based on an assumption that the so-called industrial ethics is competent of itself to cure the ills of an industrial civilization. It believes, rather, that men must be brought once more to feel their responsibility to a law within nature but not of nature in the naturalistic sense of the word. It is because Mr. Wilson and his kind can see no reality in this something not of nature, and will grant no inalienable authority to its commands, that, seeking reality, they fly distractedly from admiration of Proust to admiration of Marx.

JAMES JOYCE

[Published in the *American Review* for May 1935]

IN MR. T. S. ELIOT's latest volume of prose, *After Strange Gods,* there are several sentences that have been turning over in my memory all through the recent reading, rather re-reading, of Joyce, and have given point to my reflections. More than once Mr. Eliot and I had fallen out in conversation over that portentous author, and perhaps my reaction to these comments has a little the note of repentance, since the inability of the printed page to retort invites a degree of assent which it would be humiliating to accord to the same ideas in the heat of controversy. I refer to such statements as that Joyce's works are charged with Christian sentiment and that he is the most "orthodox" of the moderns. More particularly I have in mind the comparison of two short stories respectively by Katherine Mansfield and D. H. Lawrence with the final scene of *Dubliners* by Joyce. All three tales deal with virtually the same situation, Miss Mansfield's *Bliss* with the disillusion of a wife about her relations with her husband, Lawrence's *The Shadow in the Rose Garden* and *The Dead* of Joyce with the similar disillusion of a husband. Mr. Eliot's thesis is the difference of ethical implication. In *Bliss* he finds no hint of any perception in the author's mind of the moral issue of good and evil involved in such an awakening; in Lawrence besides such amoralism he discovers a strain of sheer alarming cruelty; whereas the disillusioned husband in Joyce has a sudden revealing glimpse of that innocent love, spiritualized by the sentiment of Christian tradition, which a long-dead boy had lavished upon his wife when a girl, and which he himself had so completely missed in his coarser physical possession:

> Generous tears filled Gabriel's eyes. He had never felt like that himself towards any woman, but he knew that such a feeling must be love. . . . His soul had approached that region where dwell the vast hosts of the dead.

And Mr. Eliot is, I now see, right. By nature Joyce was a moralist endowed with that penetration into the secret issues of life which can scarcely exist without a keen sense of religious values; and he was, indeed is, an artist gifted with genius, nothing less, for the subtleties of style. So much I am forced to admit. My fault was that, annoyed by the obliquities of his latest manner, I judged his work as a whole without historical discrimination. Now my dilemma is to explain by what experience of life and by what theories of art a man capable, when barely more than a youth, of writing the last scene of *The Dead,* should have been brought to wallow in the moral slough of *Ulysses* and to posture through the linguistic impertinences of *Work in Progress.*

I

The answer to that question must be sought in *A Portrait of the Artist as a Young Man,* which followed the collection of short stories in the *Dubliners,* and under the name of Stephen Dedalus gives a thinly disguised account of Joyce's own preparation for the career of literature. It is a work of mixed value. A good deal of the conversation of the group of students surrounding Stephen is still to me cheaply sordid and irritatingly disjointed; but for the most part the book justifies Mr. Eliot's praise of the author as one permeated with Catholic sentiment, and it contains passages of really exquisite prose. For the latter I need only mention the famous picture of the bathing girl (p. 199 of the edition in the Modern Library), beyond which few writers of English have gone in conveying the glamour of human flesh untainted by lust.

But behind these glimpses of haunting grace, mingled, it must be admitted, with scenes of satyr-like ugliness, runs the story of Stephen's conversion from religion to art. The boy is brought up in a family devoutly Catholic and intensely Irish; and in a sense Joyce himself, though he has rebelled against both these restrictions, has never lost the stamp they set upon his soul. Now it is to be noted that the religious atmosphere enveloping his formative years was mediaeval to a degree hard for one moulded by other ideas to comprehend. Such a survival from the dead past was indeed not without aesthetic appeal to the imagination, but it was shot through with materialistic magic carried straight down from the Darkest Ages. It calls for a faith capable of creating saints, but it offers little support—certainly so, as presented by Joyce; I am not at all criticising Roman Catholicism itself—for the sober integrities of daily conduct, and provides little power to resist the corrosions of modern rationalism. And we must note also that his Ireland was of the sordid, down-at-the-heels kind

which puts away the unliked obligations of life with
a jest and has furnished too easy a target for caricature. What the *Portrait* gives us, then, is the story
of one who is escaping from the demands of a religion
compounded of mediaevalism and patriotism into the
alluring liberty of pure art. Stephen is educated by
Jesuits and is expected to become a priest. A vein of
subtle psychology runs through his earlier analyses
of religious experience, showing us that we are not
far from the *Dubliners;* but even here there is already
something, I will not say of insincerity, but of sentimental religiosity. What really enthralls him is a
luxury of emotion, Christian in its conviction of sin
and its vision of purity, which yet fails of conversion
into character. His temptation is primarily of the
imagination. The supernatural element of an inherited
ritualism dissolves more and more, as we proceed, into the thin vapours of the body. And so, in that scene
of morning reverie as he lies in bed (pp. *259 ff.*), we
are not surprised to find recollections of the confes-
sional and radiant images of the eucharist melting
into dreams of the flesh:

> Her nakedness yielded to him, radiant, warm odorous and
> lavish limbed, enfolded him like a shining cloud, enfolded him
> like water with a liquid life: and like a cloud of vapour or like
> waters circumfluent in space the liquid letters of speech, symbols
> of the element of mystery, flowed forth over his brain.

So far it is not so much a matter of formal disbelief
as of spiritual lapse. The actual conversion to intellectual doubt, the second temptation, seems to have
been brought about by a series of sermons on the four
"last things": death, judgement, heaven, hell. In part
the tragic effect on the sensitive hearer was produced
by the Jesuit preacher's insistence on evil as a disease

eating into the very substance of the soul, but in greater part by his presentation of the future life of the damned in terms of materialistic horror brought straight out of the Dark Ages. Upon Stephen the first impression was purely emotional: "The faint glimmer of fear became a terror of spirit as the hoarse voice of the preacher blew death into his soul. He suffered its agony." I do not know how far these sermons, which make the centre of the book and are reported with extraordinary vividness, are authentic, and how far a dramatization of what was going on slowly in the author's mind. In either case they show, I think, how the shock of frightful threats out of the other-world acted to tear religion and art asunder. There could be no comfortable coalescence of religious symbols, however devoid of spiritual authority, with kindred vapours of the flesh until the dogmas of faith were rejected categorically by the intellect. Only so could the imagination be freed of responsibility to any power save its own untrammelled creativity.

And to these negative influences were added others of a more positive sort. There was the author's pure delight in the charm of language. He is haunted by a chance phrase: "A day of dappled seaborne clouds." He meditates on the power of words to convey the flowing scenery of the outer world; and from this turns to their more intimate connection with the flood of thoughts and images passing spontaneously through his own soul: "He drew less pleasure from the reflection of the glowing sensible world through the prism of a language manycoloured and richly storied than from the contemplation of an inner world of individual emotions mirrored perfectly in a lucid supple periodic prose." And then follows that vision of the bathing girl, so exquisitely recorded, with its promise that in art he should indeed discover a sphere for the imagination, where rhythm and beauty may be pursued for their own sweet sake, freed from any such external demand upon the conscience as had driven him from religion. Stephen's reflections on this ideal of art, in conversation with a fellow student, are mixed with half-digested scraps from the aesthetic theories of Aristotle and St. Thomas Aquinas and show that disjointed sort of erudition always dear to Joyce's vanity; but in the main they are sound enough.

And so, at the close of the book, in a sentence from Stephen's diary which has perhaps been more admired than anything else from Joyce's pen, we have the artist's viaticum: "Welcome, O life! I go to encounter for the millionth time the reality of experience and to forge in the smithy of my soul the uncreated conscience of my race." Into that noble purpose, as it appears, have been converted the religion and nationalism which had held him in bondage. Art has set him free. And the result is *Ulysses*.

II

Now in what I have to say about that extraordinary book, I would first of all acknowledge my indebtedness to Mr. Stuart Gilbert's analytical commentary, which seems to me, however I may disagree with its animating purpose, one of the most helpful and intelligent guides I have ever read to a difficult piece of literature. In chapter after chapter it brings out meanings and intentions which I should have missed in my impatient perusal, but which I find authenticated by reference to the original. And it has behind it the authority of Joyce himself, "to whose assistance and encouragement," as the writer avows, his "work owes whatever of merit it may possess." To those who find *Ulysses* impossible reading yet would know what it is all about, I recommend Mr. Gilbert's volume as an easy and fairly adequate substitute.

In brief, *Ulysses* is the story of a single day in the life of one Leopold Bloom, a Jewish canvasser of advertisements in Dublin, beginning with his preparation of early breakfast for his wife in bed, following him through the city in his wanderings and occasional transactions of business, bringing him back home late at night, and ending with the half-awake and chiefly erotic musings of his wife as she lies again in bed. Crossing this journey of Odysseus-Bloom runs the divagation of Stephen Dedalus, the hero of the earlier *Portrait,* now a school-teacher and writer, who has left the house of his natural father, a pitiable example of Irish fecklessness, as Joyce sees his beloved countrymen, and is in search of a true father in the spirit, *i.e.,* Bloom. That is the thread of the narrative; but it is entangled, lost here to reappear there, in the chance meetings of a host of other vagabonds, whose talk for the most part is in the language of the gutter. And all this takes place in the labyrinth of Dublin streets and houses, a kind of reeling kaleidoscope of fragmentary images which might with some justice be regarded as the true theme of the book.

The narrative, if such it may be called, is divided into eighteen sections, the first three of which are introductory, and deal with the setting-forth of Telemachus-Dedalus in search of a father and his meeting with a Nestor and a Proteus. Follows the body of the story of Bloom in twelve episodes, which bear some resemblance to the adventures of Odysseus with Calypso, the Lotus-eaters, Hades, Aeolus (a newspaper office), the Lestrygonians, etc., etc. The conclusion is again divided into three sections: Eumaeus (Bloom's rescue of Stephen in a drunken brawl), Ithaca (Bloom's return with Stephen to his home), and Penelope (Mrs. Bloom's neurotic reverie in bed).

It may appear far-fetched to describe Bloom's successive adventures in Dublin as an *Odyssey,* and indeed the relation to Homer's tale is often indicated, at least for the casual reader, by such stray allusions as the disgusting table-manners of the diners in a restaurant, which may recall the filthy feeding of the Lestrygonians; or the first words of the Citizen in the Cyclops episode, who is telling how "I was . . . at the corner of Arbour hill there and be damned but a bloody sweep came along and he near drove his gear into my eye." More characteristic of this artificial association, and indeed of Joyce's method generally, is the Wandering Rocks. This is but a brief incident in Homer, as it stands in Worseley's translation:

> . . . there wild rocks upswell
> Vast, overshadowing, round whose bases cry
> Dark Amphitrite's billows. Gods on high
> These rocks call Wanderers; and no wingèd thing
> That place hath passed, or can pass, harmless by.

In *Ulysses* there is motion aplenty, and to spare, and in this particular episode the meetings of person with person jump about from street to street and from shop to shop in a manner to bewilder even a hardened reader. But what the Rocks of Homer have to do with all this, it is not easy to guess—beyond the epithet "wandering." If any classical analogy is to be sought for such a maelstrom of incidents, the connecting thread of which can be known only to the author, if to him, it would be with the dance of the Lucretian atoms in the void. It is true that the name of Nausicaa can be attached with a little more propriety to the episode of the three girls on the beach. But even here it is to be observed that the opening scene, if decent, is flat and commonplace (flat and commonplace because decent, one is tempted to say), with no vestige of the charm of Homer's princess sporting with her comrades; that the shy attraction of Nausicaa to the romantically appearing hero is utterly debased in the following pornographic account of Gerty's wiles to seduce Bloom (suddenly revealed like Odysseus from his concealment), and that the meditations of Odysseus are hideously caricatured by the debauched soliloquy of Bloom when finally he is left alone. In one section only is the spirit of Homer's allegory preserved, the Circe. Bloom is determined to watch over Stephen who, in the preceding episode, had gone out staggering drunk from an orgy in Burke's public-house. To quote Mr. Gilbert's summary:

It is a misty night after the downpour and Mr. Bloom loses sight of Stephen at the entrance to nighttown. He presses on resolutely through the mist, past spectral shadows, drunken harpies, rowdy soldiers, lurching workmen, and finally comes upon Stephen in the house of Mrs. Bella Cohen in Tyrone Street. Stephen and Lynch, in the company of the prostitutes Zoe, Flora, and Kitty, are engaged in a rambling discourse on the philosophy of music; Stephen is strumming "empty fifths" on the brothel piano. Mrs. Bella Cohen demands her fees; Stephen, with fuddled generosity, exceeds the tariff, but Bloom comes to the rescue.

In the phantasmagoric visions of his former delin-
quencies that pursue Bloom while searching for his
"spiritual son," and in the transformations of the
brothel scenes, there is more than a hint of the black
magic of lust from which Odysseus saved his comrades in the enchanted island of Circe; but Homer's
poetic symbolism springs from a philosophy beyond
the ken of the modern imitator.

Apart from this last episode, itself a doubtful exception, to any one who goes through *Ulysses* with
the *Odyssey* fresh in mind, *experto crede,* the vaunted
parallelism between the two works is thoroughly
superficial. Nor can I see any grounds for taking
seriously Mr. Louis Golding's theory that the wanderings of the Homeric Odysseus have been converted
into "a commentary on the evolution of mankind
from its heroic beginnings to its present weary conditions."[1] There are to be sure a few allusions to the
ancient civilization of Ireland and other odd bits of
antiquarian lore scattered about; there is, for one
reader at least, abundant weariness in the life of
Joyce's Dublin, which may, if one chooses, be contrasted with the heroism of ancient Greece; but of
historic evolution, such as Mr. Golding imagines, I
see nothing. And I should hate to believe that three
thousand years have brought to mankind only weariness and ugliness from which no escape is possible
save in a weary and ugly art.

III

The evolution that interests the critic is of another
and less grandiose kind. We have seen the national-

[1] *James Joyce's Ulysses,* p. 95.

ism and Christian sentiment of the *Dubliners* slipping
over in the *Portrait* to a theory of irresponsible art, of
art for art's sake, with its goal set upon producing
pure beauty and upon forging out of the reality of
experience the uncreated conscience of the artist's
people; and now we see the execution of this ideal
in the prodigy of *Ulysses*. I do not overlook the fact
that there are dispersed fragments in the later book
of such rhythmic beauty as gave charm to parts of
the *Portrait* before the theory of pure art was carried
fully into practice; but as a whole the realization of
art in *Ulysses* is a creation of ugliness, a congeries of
ugly pictures expressed in the speech of Dublin's gut-
ters. What has happened? Here, I think, we can elimi-
nate the factor of nationalism, which remains fairly
constant from the beginning to the end of Joyce's
career; the changing factor is the self-liberation of
the artist from the spiritual values and dogmatic
authority of tradition, and the consequent forging
of "conscience" out of the uncontrolled spontaneity
of his individual consciousness. Here in the main
Joyce was but following the path from symbolism
to "naturism" in France which recently has been so
ably expounded by Marcel Raymond in his essay on
the movement *De Baudelaire au surréalisme,* and
which, stopping short of superrealism (we are looking for a parallel with *Ulysses,* not with *Work in
Progress*), came to a climax in the fiction of Proust.
And it may be noted by the way, merely as a curious
fact, that the three acknowledged fathers of this general movement are Americans—Poe and Whitman
and Henry James.

The point is that the pursuit of art as an abstraction divorced from the responsibilities of life leads to nothing, and idealistic beauty loosed from belief in the higher reality of spiritual ideas is no more than a mist fluttering in the infinite inane. And the imagination of man, his whole soul, craves reality. The artist who sets out to capture that phantom ideal is like a man in a balloon when his moorings are cut. He soars upward and upward until the air about him grows too thin to breathe, and the chill temperature benumbs his blood, and in the great height above the solidities of earth and the comfortable contacts of humanity he is overtaken by an awful dizziness of the void. He deflates the balloon and falls rushing downwards. The aeronaut may land safely on the ground from which he rose. But for the artist there is rarely such a return. In his reactionary search for reality he is precipitated down and down into the depths of his own being, into that vast dark region of the soul below the plain of ordered and rationalized life. Being unable to sink lower he will feel that at last his feet are set on a foundation of facts which he calls the nature of man. His art will be to reproduce in flowing language the vapours that float up unsolicited through the conscious mind from that abyss of the unconscious. Rational selection and spiritual authority have been repudiated, and the only law governing the flux is the so-called association of ideas, the fact that one image by some chance similarity evokes another, and one sensation fades into another. In this way the artist who sets out to forge the "conscience" of his people ends in identifying this with the so-called "stream of consciousness" into which his own soul has been dissolved. Why it should be so may perhaps be beyond our comprehension, but the truth remains that sheer ugliness and morbid perversions abound in this stream from the bottom of man's being. With Proust this meant that the ultimate reality of human experience is reached in the horrors of sadism and masochism. In *Ulysses,* perhaps owing to the hangover from a more religious training, perhaps to other causes, these vices are not conspicuous; but the root of ugliness is there and constantly recurring hints of sexual abnormality of another, if less cruel, sort.

Now the result of this spontaneous association of ideas may appear in either one of two forms. It may produce such spasmodic imagery as we saw in the episodes of The Wandering Rocks and Circe and indeed in the greater part of *Ulysses,* or it may flow continuously from image to image, and from memory to memory, and from desire to desire, as in the final episode where Mrs. Bloom's dreaming meditations are written out in page after page without punctuation. For the reader, who would trace the law of association governing the stream, this is hard going, indeed a harder book to read than *Ulysses* you will scarcely find, unless it be Joyce's own later fragments of *Work in Progress,* or some of the *surréaliste* vagaries which emanate from the same school of naturalistic art gone mad.

Why then do our fiercer "intellectuals" devote to the study of *Ulysses,* as in fact some of them do, an amount of study which they would disdain to apply to Plato or Aristotle or the Bible? I believe that two causes are here at work. For the first there is a prodigious amount of sheer intellection behind *Ulysses.*

This attempt to give expression to the stream of consciousness is not the outcome of haphazard writing, but is the product of a brain busily engaged in detecting and utilizing the association of ideas directing the flow. Such brain-work is not the creative power of a mind choosing out of the given mass of upsurging ideas those that can be formed into a noble pattern of life, but an intense concentration upon the currents and counter-currents, the sudden novelties and the repeated successions, just as these emerge into the light. And there is the inborn mastery of language to clothe in appropriate words each emergent image or situation as it is seen. The mere range of Joyce's vocabulary devoted to the expression of the undercurrents of life has an almost inexhaustible attraction for the student of literary technique. For myself I have the impression that in this exploitation of the subconscious spontaneity of association Joyce displays a penetration and intelligence greater than that which made Proust famous, whether this be due to his earlier training in religious psychology or to native genius. And the disciple who will bestow upon *Ulysses* the time and concentration required for comprehending the procedure of the author's mind has all the excitement of superior enlightenment.

The pleasure is there and real, to pick up if you care enough for that sort of thing; but its nature may be, and by the devotees of Joyce commonly is, mistaken. It is not, in itself, the joy of art. I do not mean to sever art as a pure abstraction from other activities of the mind; but I would insist that the difficulty of grasping the ideas of great literature involves an elevation of the will and the emotions in which this

detective pursuit of difficulties plays a very subordinate rôle. That is certainly true of the *Odyssey* as
compared with *Ulysses*. Nor is the excitement of
unravelling Joyce's method the same as that which
may accompany the mastery of an artist who is also
a great scholar. There is indeed a certain display of
erudition in the composition of *Ulysses*; but it is of
a disorganized sort, tags out of St. Thomas and
Aristotle dispersed among floating allusions to very
modern theories of psychology and aesthetics, with
no comprehension of any one of the great systems
of thought and no sense of the concatenated tradition of philosophy. Mr. Gilbert makes much of the
Oriental, particularly the Hindu, element in *Ulysses*;
but if this be examined it will appear to rest on the
uncritical reading of such charlatans as Mme. Blavat-
sky and Mr. Sinnett—facile references to transmigration and nirvana and the growing soul-ego, which can
only bring a smile to any one who has drunk deeply
of the genuine springs of Orientalism. They remind
me of an incident of my own youth. I had got the
first volume of *Isis Unveiled* from the local library,
but inquiry after inquiry for the second volume always brought from the girl at the desk, a friend of
mine, the reply that it was out. At last, seeing and
admiring my eagerness, she broke the rules of the
library, and kept the book hidden for me when next
it was turned in. And so I was able to finish that
masterpiece of theosophy. "And what did you think
of the book?" she asked when I brought back the
second volume.—"It interested me," I answered, "but
annoyed me too because I couldn't make out what it
was all about."—"Oh," said she, leaning over the

desk and speaking in a mysterious whisper, "you are not supposed to understand it!"

No, the pleasure of the intellect that infatuates the ordinary partisan of *Ulysses* has little to do with thought in the larger sense of the word. It is the vanity of guessing why one incident succeeds another, where to the casual reader the connection seems purely arbitrary; or it is the satisfaction of grasping quickly that "Blmstup" is a humpty-dumpty compression for "Bloom stood up," or that "monstruosity" is shorthand for "monstrosity-abstrusity" (this I love), or of filling out the innumerable examples of aposiopesis, or of guessing the sense of a phrase or sentence which is perfectly blank until one goes back to it after pages of patient reading. To illustrate this last point I may quote the opening lines of The Sirens:

> Bronze by gold heard the hoofirons, steelyringing.
> Imperthnthn thnthnthn.
> Chips, picking chips off rocky thumbnail, chips.
> Horrid! And gold flushed more.
> A husky fifenote blew.
> Blew. Blue bloom is on the
> Gold pinnacled hair.

And so on and on and on. Mr. Gilbert admits that these pages are "almost meaningless" (why the "almost"?) until the reader has pursued the chapter to the end. But he regards the whole thing as a supreme achievement of " 'atonement' between subject-matter and form":

> This episode differs from most examples of "musical prose" in that the meaning does not lose but is, rather, intensified by the combination of the two arts; sense is not sacrificed to sound but the two are so harmonized that, unless his ears, like the

Achaeans', are sealed with wax against the spell, the reader, hearkening to "the voice sweet as the honeycomb and having joy thereof, will go on his way the wiser."

To me, as I suspect it will be to most readers, the notion that wisdom is to be got out of all this mystification looks like an act of artistic faith beyond anything required by the mysteries of religion. But I admit that, if you like that sort of thing and have nothing else to think about, the puzzle of getting sense out of apparent nonsense may have its reward.

If this were all one might dismiss the champions of *Ulysses* as mere cranks, endowed with a restless brain and cursed with nothing to think about—and such there are, I am sure, among the sanctified band. But there is something else. The book has another attraction arising out of its *forense* (if I may make a feeble addition to the Joycean lingo), to explain which an exposition must be added of Joyce's, and his admirers', aesthetic philosophy. In a notable passage of the *Portrait* a sharp distinction was drawn between what the author describes as the "kinetic" and the "static" aim of art, terms which he connects with Aristotle's famous definition of tragedy in the *Poetics,* and which are so important for his practice as well as his theory that I must quote his argument at some length. Stephen Dedalus, the embryonic artist of the *Portrait* and the spokesman there and in *Ulysses* for the author himself, is talking with a fellow student named Lynch:

—Pity is the feeling which arrests the mind in the presence of whatsoever is grave and constant in human sufferings and unites it with the human sufferer. Terror is the feeling which arrests the mind in the presence of whatsoever is grave and constant in human sufferings and unites it with the secret cause.—

—Repeat—said Lynch.

Stephen repeated the definition slowly. . . .

—The tragic emotion, in fact, is a face looking two ways, towards terror and towards pity, both of which are phases of it. You see I use the word *arrest*. I mean that the tragic emotion is static. Or rather the dramatic emotion is. The feelings excited by improper art are kinetic, desire or loathing. Desire urges us to possess, to go to something; loathing urges us to abandon, to go from something. The arts which excite them, pornographical or didactic, are therefore improper arts. The aesthetic emotion (I used the general term) is therefore static. The mind is arrested and raised above desire and loathing.—

Now so taken, with the right qualifications, this distinction between kinetic and static is, I hold, sound and fundamental. The moment literature aims to move, to be kinetic of, the *physical* sense of desire and loathing—to rouse the lustful passions, to produce horror of the nerves (as for example the actual nausea of altitude stirred by the fall of Frollo in Victor Hugo's *Notre Dame*), to effect bodily shrinking from the loathsome (as in much of the post-War literature)—that moment, whatever its excuse as propaganda, it ceases to be art, or becomes bad art, which is the same thing. And Joyce goes on to connect this thesis with his conception of rhythm and beauty:

—Beauty expressed by the artist cannot awaken in us an emotion which is kinetic or a sensation which is purely physical. It awakens, or ought to awaken, or induces, or ought to induce, an aesthetic stasis, an ideal pity or an ideal terror, a stasis called forth, prolonged and at last dissolved by what I call the rhythm of beauty.—

That, in its first intention, I believe, is a noble theory of art, nobly stated, and if carried out with Joyce's native endowment of genius, might have enriched literature with a masterpiece of beauty. But upon this theory there is superimposed another view of art which has led to confusion of ideas in the

Portrait and to worse confusion of execution in
Ulysses. According to this superimposed theory, derived not at all from Aristotle or from classical practice but from romantic naturalism, stasis acquires an
independent meaning of its own, beyond the mere
opposition to the wrong sort of kinesis. Static art
should not only refrain from exciting the physical
sensations of desire and loathing, it should not merely
avoid immorality, but should aim to be neither im-
moral nor moral by maintaining the complete "indifference of nature" towards what is seen, and by
reproducing the facts of nature with a realism that
eschews any attempt at interpretation. So it is that
the romantic notion of art for art's sake, set loose
from any responsibility to the authority of spiritual
law and traditional inhibitions, merges into a naturalism which rejects from reality all but the physical and
in the end all but the ugly.

Now this romantic-naturalistic theory of art which
Mr. Gilbert has developed with much acumen in the
first chapter of his commentary, does give a veracious
account of what such writers as Proust and Joyce
have sought to accomplish and to a degree have accomplished. But to designate this accomplishment as
"realism"—if by that one means that such artists
have represented the bare facts, and all the facts, of
life without selective interpretation—is to fall into
gross misunderstanding that borders on stark nonsense; it even gives to stasis a meaning utterly incon-
sistent with Joyce's own use of the word as formally
distinguished from kinesis. The simple truth is that
all literature, except perhaps the humblest and least
pretentious kind of fiction, is interpretative, and as

such is kinetic, in so far as it is creative. Homer was not only interpreting, but more or less purposely re-shaping, the earlier Greek notions of life and religion. Virgil was consciously, for a purpose, interpreting the facts of Roman history. And there is no need to pursue this argument down through the names of Dante and Cervantes and Shakespeare and Milton and Racine and Voltaire and Goethe. What I would enforce is the point that Joyce's *Ulysses* is not at all the sort of realism which he and his critic Gilbert take it to be, but is in the fullest measure an inter-pretation of what the world and life are in accord-ance with a particular philosophy of life and under the sway of a particular philosophy of reality; that he worked out this interpretation with extraordinary industry and cunning; that his claim to a place in the higher region of literature depends not on a supposed realism but on his interpretation of reality, and that it is assent to the highly kinetic philosophy under-lying this interpretation which enthralls most at least of his rather simple-minded devotees and explains their zestful expenditure of labour.

To bring these conclusions back to the theory of art expounded by Joyce in the *Portrait,* I should say that the initial error there was one of terminology. He would have formulated his principles more cor-rectly if, instead of a contrast between kinetic and static, he had distinguished between art that aims to arouse physical lust or loathing and art that seeks to move desire and joy of hyperphysical realities; for all art, so far as it is alive, must be kinetic. And then, by identifying stasis with naturalistic "realism," he has rendered his art kinetic in precisely the sense he started out to avoid.

IV

Now the naturalistic philosophy behind Joyce's art is in itself simple enough, and indeed is already obvious in what has been said of his psychology, being nothing more than a theory of objective reality which will correspond to the inner stream of consciousness. As that view of the soul was attained by liberating the ego from any spiritual authority not itself, and from any selective law of reason within itself, so the field of visible phenomena and of physical events, amid which the soul plays its part, shall be freed from the governance of any transcendent power and from any principle of order within itself. To the irrational association of ideas shall correspond a conception of nature as an accidental succession of emergencies, and the irresponsibility of conscience shall be the mirror of a world which merely is what it is.

And what of the theoretical distinction of kinetic and static art when put to the test of reality so conceived? Some light, I think, will be shed upon this question by the "monumental decision of the United States district court rendered December 6, 1933, by the Hon. John M. Woolsey, lifting the ban on *Ulysses*," which is prefixed to the American edition of the book. Judge Woolsey's decree is based on literary and moral grounds. For the first he sees clearly enough the artistic method of the work:

Joyce has attempted—it seems to me with astonishing success —to show how the screen of consciousness with its ever-shifting kaleidoscopic impressions carries, as it were on a plastic palimpsest, not only what is in the focus of each man's observation of the actual things about him, but also in a penumbral zone residua of past impressions, some recent and some drawn up by association from the domain of the subconscious. He shows how each of these impressions affects the life and behaviour of the character which he is describing.

And the judge's ethical acquittal is given in the belief that the execution of this method, though "in many places it seems to" him "to be disgusting," is neither "pornographic" nor "obscene."

Now we may grant that *Ulysses* as a whole is not pornographic, if by that term we mean an intent "to stir the sex impulses or to lead to sexually impure and lustful thoughts." To this extent the book is not kinetic in the Joycean conception, though for myself I cannot see how certain isolated passages, as for example Gerty's seductive wiles in the Nausicaa episode already referred to, can be relieved of such an imputation. But the case stands otherwise if we consider the word "obscene." Judge Woolsey seems to make no distinction between pornography and obscenity, and indeed the above-given definition of pornography is cited by him from an earlier legal decision in regard to the obscene. But however it may be in law, are the words actually synonymous? Is not obscenity a more general term signifying what is foul, what excites disgust? And if Judge Woolsey is right in holding that the book in many places is disgusting, then, by Joyce's own definition of kinetic as that which moves the reader to loathing as well as to lust, is not the art of *Ulysses* on this side kinetic, rather than static, and so bad art?

I do not see how, by the author's own definition, his work can escape this condemnation; indeed, in de-

tail after detail, he would seem to have gone out of
his way to introduce the note of obscenity with the
direct aim of exciting disgust of the loathsome. We
have seen how in the Lestrygonians he exhausts all
his resources to describe the bare act of eating in a
manner almost to produce physical nausea. But the
climax of this intention comes in the Hades episode,
where the unclean circumstances of death are gloated
over with a horrible fascination suggestive of the sort
of nightmare that might haunt the sleep of one who,
by the favour of a knowing undertaker, has gazed
upon what ordinarily is hidden from the eye. And
then the graveyard:

> An obese grey rat toddled along the side of the crypt, moving
> the pebbles. An old stager: great-grandfather: he knows the
> ropes. The grey alive crushed itself in under the plinth, wriggling
> itself in under it. Good hidingplace for treasure. . . .

There is worse than that, much worse; things that
the normal human mind would never imagine and
that it would be a pollution to quote.

But these details of tumescent filth are only symp-
toms of an inwardly corroding disease. The realism,
of which Joyce's admirers make so much, springs
from a belief, not the less devastating because perfectly arbitrary, that reality must be sought in what
lies below the surface of appearances, what lies above
having been expunged as a delusion of authority. The
living man as a vehicle of the soul is not a real thing,
but only the putrid corpse; the body as it appears to
the eye is not a real thing, but to know its reality
you must strip it of its integument and fumble in its
entrails. And this identification of realism with the
under side of nature is the almost inevitable companion of an atheistic philosophy that dissolves the uni-

verse into a Protean flux of meaningless change. The
bottom of things, the darkness from which the sun is
excluded, is verminous. As Mr. Gilbert says of a scene
in the Scylla and Charybdis,

. . . we feel a tensity of cerebration that is almost pain in Stephen's dialectical progress towards a paradoxical conclusion, the
cul de sac of a mystery. On that mystery the book *Ulysses,* all
religion and every explanation of the universe is founded—"upon
the void. Upon incertitude, upon unlikelihood." This spirit of incertitude is materialized in the Circe episode, where phantoms
of the "feast of pure reason"—Shakespeare among them—gesticu-
late mechanically, inane puppets, in a *danse macabre.*

Whether this philosophy of the inane, where ugliness
breeds spontaneously, is a consequence of a psychology which dissolves conscience into the stream of
consciousness, or whether the genetic order is the
reverse, I should not care to say. In either case
obscenity becomes a kind of substitute for the ideals
of religion, a despotic faith in the horror of utter disorder behind the illusion of decency and stability.
There is thus no reason to be surprised at the strange
inverted reminiscences of Joyce's early Catholicism
that come here and there to the surface of his naturalism.

The book opens with a mocking intonation of the
Introibo ad altare Dei, and the preface to any particularly polluted incident is likely to be some other
tag from the liturgy of the Church. Hints of the
eucharist abound, the climax of the blasphemous
parody coming at the wildest moment of the brothel
scene, when a Black Mass is celebrated, with anti-
phonal voices of the Damned and the Blessed, and the
sacred words are read backwards: "Htengier Tneto-
pinmo Dog Drol eht rof, Aiulella!"

It is this religion *à rebours* in *Ulysses,* this faith in
the final reality of nature as something so loathsome
that man is relieved of the burden of loyalty to any
authority outside himself, and is left to revel in his
own sense of superiority—it is this, behind the joy of
"a tensity of cerebration," I would assert, that fasci-
nates a certain type of modernist—above all the
vanity of the illusion of irresponsibility.

V

To Mr. Eliot the bitter realization of obscenity in
Joyce—and there is bitterness beneath his rollicking
audacity—gives to his work the note of religious
"orthodoxy" based on the conviction of sin. To me,
I will confess, this spectacle of a great genius expend-
ing itself on the propagation of irresponsibility, while
the fabric of society is shaken to its foundation,
brings rather dismay and sadness. With Mr. Eliot I
disagree reluctantly, since at bottom we are, I trust
and believe, in accord; but there are those, the
"emancipated," with whom the issue is of another
sort.

Here I will for once fling caution to the winds and
speak out what I feel, though it subject me to the
retort of ribald laughter. In this art I see at work not
the conviction of sin, but the ultimate principle of evil
invoked as the very enemy of truth. And I fortify, or
rationalize, my instinctive revulsion by what I hold
would be the judgement of philosophy and theology.
For the first, what else is this exploitation of the subconscious but an attempt to reduce the world and the
life of man back to the abysmal chaos out of which,

as Plato taught, God created the actual cosmos by
the imposition of law and reason upon the primaeval
stuff of chance and disorder. And for the second
I would appeal to no formal treatise of theology but
to one of the "ghost" stories in Monsignor R. H.
Benson's *Mirror of Shalott,* which has haunted my
imagination all through the reading of Joyce.

I refer to the tale in which Father Girdlestone re-
lates the three assaults of the devil to capture his soul.
Now what first impressed me in that ghostly narration was the order in which the author arranged these
temptations, seeming to begin with the most radical
and to end with the least radical. And this apparently
inverted climax puzzled me until I saw how curiously
it corresponds with the actual progress of Joyce from
the *Portrait* to *Ulysses.* In Benson's fiction the first
temptation is "completely in the transcendent sphere";
it is an intrusion of the evil one into the priest's
spiritual dreams, "as when one's imagination is full
of some remembered melody and a real sound breaks
upon it"; it is a questioning of the validity of all
religious experience as something unreal and devoid
of authority. Then follows a more open and direct
attack upon the reason. "It was intellectual doubt of
the whole thing. . . . After all, . . . where is the
proof? What shadow of a proof is there that the
whole thing is not a dream? If there were objective
proof, how could any man doubt? If there is not objective proof, what reason have you to trust in religion at all?" And the priest adds: "A heavy deposit
had been left upon my understanding. I did not dare
to sit down and argue; I did not dare to run for

refuge to the Silence of God. I was driven out into the sole thing that was left—the world of sense."

So far we are moving parallel with what we have seen to have been the two steps in the emancipation of Stephen in the *Portrait*. And then, carrying us over to the execution of art in *Ulysses,* comes the third and deadliest assault. In the priest's story this is described as the insurgence of evil from its last and most secret lair, a voice crying to him that even the world of sense is an illusion, a whirling of shadows in the void beneath which the only reality is some horror of loathing. It is as if the solid objects about him, the very furniture of the room where his religious life had passed, were "striving to hold themselves in material being under the stress of some enormous destructive force." At times they seemed to him "to have gone, simply to have dissolved into nothingness, as a breath fades on a window—to retain but a phantom of themselves." And it was known to him that what was intended was to merge the world of sense into the very essence of evil:

I understood at this moment, as never before, how that process consummates itself. It begins, as mine did, with the carrying of the inner life by storm that may come about by deliberate acquiescence in sin—I should suppose that it always does in some degree. Then the intellect is attacked—it may only be in one point—a "delusion" it is called; and with many persons regarded only as eccentric the process goes no further. But when the triumph is complete, the world of sense too is lost—and the man raves. I knew at that time for absolute fact that this is the process. The "delusions" of the mad are not non-existent—they are glimpses, horrible or foul or fantastic, of that strange world that we take so quietly for granted, that at this moment and at every moment is perpetually about us—foaming out its waters in lust or violence or mad irresponsible blasphemy against the Most High.

That would be the report of theology on the art of the obscene, and if it seems to a certain type of reader purely arbitrary to apply such a criterion to the work of Joyce, let me recall to him the words of Stephen in the *Portrait*: "I imagine that there is a malevolent reality behind those things I say I fear."

THE MODERNISM OF FRENCH POETRY

[Published in the *American Review* for June 1935]

IN my recent study of James Joyce I made the observation that his work was in English a more or less exotic offshoot of a literary movement whose regular and logical development in France had been analysed in Marcel Raymond's *De Baudelaire au surréalisme*; and I called attention to the curious fact that the acknowledged fathers of the whole movement were three Americans: Poe and Whitman and Henry James. It has seemed to me worth while to add a few words in development of this casual comment, as a sort of pendant to that essay.

Of the primary position of these Americans there is abundant evidence in the pages of M. Raymond and of other critics in the same field. This is particularly true of Poe, as can be seen by any reader of Paul Valéry's philosophical justification of modernism in *Variété*, which not only contains various scattered allusions to Poe's influence, but devotes a long essay to the metaphysic of *Eureka*; and indeed M. Valéry is but exploiting the well-known fascination of the American poet and critic for Baudelaire, who is commonly taken as the fountain and origin of the cycle of adventures from symbolism to its present efflorescence in superrealism. In Poe's verse can be found something of that dissolution of the solid world of

phenomena into images of an inner fluctuation of the
soul which is the very essence of "symbolism," and
in his critical dissertations there is a clear exposition
of the ideal of pure poetry towards which the symbolists have all been straining. From this source came
that conception of "the rhythmical creation of beauty"
so dominant in the aesthetic theorizing of Joyce's
Portrait, with the belief that such a rhythmical evocation can be effected only when the creative genius is
liberated from any obligation to the duties and truth
of prosaic life—with the practical result, in Joyce, of
Ulysses.

Whitman's influence, though it extended to the
realm of art itself as seen in the spread of *vers libre,*
bears more directly on the philosophical, or psychological, aspect of the movement. The heart of the
matter is in the *Song of Myself,* in which two entities
are set over against each other,—the absolute Ego
and all about it the objective world which consists of
a flowing stream of impressions having in themselves
no distinction of values:

> I celebrate myself, and sing myself,
> And what I assume you shall assume,
> For every atom belonging to me as good belongs to you.
>
> .   .   .   .   .   .
>
> Creeds and schools in abeyance,
> Retiring back awhile sufficed at what they are, but never
>   forgotten,
> I harbour for good or bad, I permit to speak at every
>   hazard,
> Nature without check with original energy.

That is the creed of egoism and naturalism which
Paul Valéry was to expound as a new metaphysic of
the schools.

For the third we have the later novels of Henry James. Those who have read Percy Lubbock's subtle study of *The Craft of Fiction* need not be reminded how the originality of *The Ambassadors*, for instance, consists in laying hold of the various, often contradictory, desires and needs of an individual soul, and in presenting these as if they were almost independent actors engaged in conflict within that soul as their stage. So the traditional drama of person against person, or of person against fate, is changed into an inner clash of impersonal motives. To Mr. Lubbock this psychological drama, in which the psyche is the scene of action rather than itself an actor, is the culmination of a long movement, a climax beyond which there is no direct advance, a great but sterile art. But take from James the root of New England conscience (for that is his inheritance, whatever the place of his birth), give to each of the psychological combatants freedom and equal validity, and for the inner drama of moral issues you have exactly the mere flux of impressions, the accidental association of sentiments and desires, the so-called stream of consciousness, so aptly exploited for the purposes of later fiction and poetry. This is not a fanciful affiliation. It may be that James's example may seem to bear more on the method than on the spirit of recent art, but it is of the very nature of art that method and spirit can scarcely be dissociated. And if it be true that his primacy is less generally recognized than Whitman's, not to mention Poe's, we have nevertheless the definite statement of Gertrude Stein (who belongs to the French group we are studying), that she regarded the author of *The Ambassadors* quite definitely as her forerunner, and that he "was the first person in literature to find the way to the literary methods of the twentieth century."

Neither Poe nor Whitman, and still less James, would have been at ease among the actual symbolists and *surréalistes* of Paris. In all three of them something remained from the American tradition which held them at the border of the promised land of freedom. But it was their partial emancipation from that tradition that was seized upon and magnified by the bolder rebels of the Continent. To Baudelaire for instance Poe was the very symbol of revolt against the bourgeois conventions for which America as a whole was the type. His admiration for Poe cannot be severed from his hatred of Poe's people. Furthermore, in pointing to these immediate sources we must not forget that everything in them can be found, and found more fully developed, *i.e.,* more consciously disembarrassed of the swaddling bands of convention, in the *romantische Schule* of Germany long before the discovery of Poe by Baudelaire; but history is full of new starts, and for the leaders of the modern movement the recognized fathers were primarily Poe, and secondarily Whitman and James. The value of M. Raymond's work is that in his pages we can trace the evolution of a whole period from these beginnings —the ideal of pure art, the dualism of the absolute Ego set against an objective world deprived of any distinction of values in itself, the interacting flux of contacts between these two poles—all mapped out with the precision and clarity for which the French genius is deservedly famous.

I must be brief in my account of M. Raymond's treatise, only prefacing my remarks with the assurance that a careful reading of the book will bring its reward to those who, like myself, admit an imperfect acquaintance with the successive schools and the many authors he describes. His analysis begins with an *Introduction* in which he studies the origin and growth of French symbolism in Baudelaire and Rimbaud and Mallarmé. As distinguished from the classical writers who were frankly intellectualists, and from the poets gathered about Victor Hugo, for whom the objective world still retained something of its independent outlines, these newer romantics would eschew any knowledge and any interest which should impinge upon the pure sentiment of the Self, and would employ their imagination in converting the sensible world into bare metaphors and symbols of its shifting but autonomous moods. In doing this they made of language what Baudelaire described as an instrument of suggestive magic. "To deliver one's soul," to rediscover "the state of nature," what was this, asks M. Raymond, but the hope, if not the consequence, of an ancestral dream half drowned in the unconscious, the dream of a magical universe wherein the spirit should hold sway over phenomena freed from the intermediary authority of reason.

After this Introduction the first section of M. Raymond's treatise is entitled *Le Reflux,* or Ebb-Tide. Here, in separate chapters, he considers the various poets and critics who reacted against symbolism at the end of the last century. Among these he lists the *Romans*—Moréas, du Plessys, La Tailhède, Ernest Raynaud—who, feeling a certain foreign element in the new romanticism, cast back in a kind of archaizing fury to an earlier reform, thoroughly French, in-

stituted by Deschamps and Ronsard. Others, such as
Maurras, less narrowly national in their search for
l'antique renom latin des Gaules, looked abroad for a
renewal of the classical tradition. These symbolists,
declared Maurras, have surrendered the classical and
French sense of style, which consists not so much in
charging words with colour and music and in using
them to convey an *état d'âme* more or less evanescent,
as in imposing order and movement upon thought,
and in subjecting thought to the higher reason.

Then follows a chapter on *La Poésie du jeune
siècle* (the twentieth), led by Régnier, Viélé-Griffin,
Verhaeren, Francis Jammes, and others, who pro-
fessedly were continuators of the naturalistic romanticism discarded by the *Romans,* but sought to combine with it a sort of humanism which should embrace
"the whole of life" and effect a reconciliation with
the modern world more realistically conceived. Yet
withal the air of poetry must not be divorced from
the poet's *prestige d'être soi.*

Passing over the chapters on *Le Réveil de la pensée
méridionale* and on the renewal of nationalism *Sous
le signe de Minerve casquée,* we reach the second section of the book entitled *A la recherche d'un nouvel
ordre français,* the chapters of which we need not
follow in detail, but content ourselves with picking
out such points as the conflict between Abbé Bremond's attempt to humiliate pure poetry before the religious mysticism of Christianity with Jean Royère's
contrary elevation of poetry to an independence of its
own: "Symbolism was nothing but the will to penetrate to the very essence of poesy"; and "The poets
who formed the generation of symbolists have all re-

garded their art as an absolute." Here belong the philosophy of the absolute Ego as propounded by Paul
Valéry, and Claudel's mystical realism; and here are
included the group of Unanimistes, Whitmaniens,
Poètes de l'Abbaye, the "Men of Good Will," who
developed a sort of "post-naturalism" in which the
more frankly egocentric naturalism is masqued under
the colours of democratic and socialistic ideology.

But I fear this cataloguing résumé is becoming a
bore, and I must deal more succinctly with the next
section of M. Raymond's history in which he gathers
together, under the general head of *L'aventure et la
révolte,* the poets more faithful to the initial impulse
of symbolism. Here we find associated in a kind of
snarling comity two distinct groups of adventurous
rebels. On the one side were those who turned from
the traditional search for an unworldly beauty to a
glorification of the hard facts of materialism, as
Marinetti announced in the programme of 1909: The
poet of the future will chant only the multi-coloured
and polyphonic revolutions in our modern capitals,
the nocturnal vibration of the dockyards and sheds
under their glaring electric lights, the railway stations
and factories, etc. On the other side are those who
denounce any attempt to express the phenomenal
world by clear ideas in favour of a general anti-
intellectualism; or who reject the traditional appearance of objects for some theory of pure vision in the
manner of the cubists; or in despair of truth end by
renouncing any sort of choice or order among the
chaos of impressions, hoping that somehow, even if
in his own despite, the poet's verse will attain to
some sort of significance. It is but a step from such a

despairing hope to the clownish school of Dadaists, who mocked at the idea of any transmissible meaning whatsoever. We have arrived at the threshold of *surréalisme,* a name first adopted, I believe, by Guillaume Apollinaire.

There is variety enough in the methods of the self-styled *surréalistes,* and indeed what else could be expected of a party of avowed rebels against authority. But there is also a certain unanimity derived from the very principle of revolt. In the manifesto of 1924 they declare their aim to be "a psychical automatism by which one proposes to express, whether orally or by writing or in any other manner, the real functioning of thought (*pensée*) as a spontaneous dictation, in the absence of any control exercised by reason and apart from any preoccupation whether aesthetic or ethical." Such an automatic communication can be effective only under the most favourable conditions: the would-be poet must abstract himself from all surrounding actuality, close so far as possible the gates of the senses that open upon the exterior world, lull reason to sleep so as to maintain himself in a state like dreaming, and then listen (but without any conscious effort of the will), and write, as thought flows in upon him.

Such is the theory of *surréalisme.* And a very little reflection will show that, for one thing, it rests on a complete confusion of terms. The hard distinctions of nature as these appear to the normal (*bourgeois*) mind are, in the Bergsonian vocabulary, a product of the falsifying reason; and the first procedure of the poet is to repudiate this distinguishing faculty for a trancelike state in which impressions of the outer world float about like shadowy forms incessantly melting one into the other. The images grasped by the imagination are metaphorical by virtue of a certain magical principle of identity. To call this automatic vision of fleeting forms thought (*pensée*) is an abuse of terms. And so of the term superrealism. Every *surréaliste* text presupposes a return to chaos, in the bosom of which a vague something called supernature automatically sketches itself as it were a thin filigree on the substratum of being. In fact this evocation of a superrealistic world ordinarily appears as a coalescence of undistinguished impressions from without with the emanations that float like vapours from the psychical substratum of the unconscious. All which is an attempt to discover reality not in what is above but in what is below nature. It is the last gasping fury of romanticism as formulated by the German mind and coloured by a century of revolt from things as they are. It is the essence of pure poetry proclaimed by Poe and adopted by Baudelaire, released now from the clinging remnants of conscience and reason. *Surréalisme* is no more than symbolism come to its own.

Before trying to get at the final significance of this evolution, which M. Raymond has analysed so adroitly, yet so far as principles are concerned so uncritically, we must first take account of the interpretation of its more immediate source on the Freudian hypothesis as expounded, *e.g.*, by Dr. René Laforgue in *L'Echec de Baudelaire*. Now the work of Dr. Laforgue I should describe as an arbitrary mixture of insight and baseless theory, of critical acumen and pseudo-science. To illustrate what I mean by this, I would refer to a passage on page 158:

Let us not forget that Baudelaire always refused to follow any profession. He wished to remain free at any price, though by doing so he must resign himself to be only king of a desert. For him evolution, growth, of any sort, was equivalent to an act of infidelity. To understand how completely the bourgeois life could mean for him something infamous, it is sufficient to consider his family situation. To succeed signified for him the capability of realizing an honest career (*une vie honnête*), like that of his stepfather, General Aupick. Such a life implied the duty of succeeding a father with whom he should identify himself, and whose place he should in some manner supplant. This rivalry of the son with his father,—we know how Baudelaire liquidated it so as not to feel guilty of desiring the death of his father. Yet he had desired just this, and had, so to speak, provoked it in his thoughts.

Now, as we shall see, the desire of freedom at any cost was fundamental to Baudelaire's whole career as a man and as an artist, but Dr. Laforgue immediately connects this with the so-called Oedipus complex of Freud, and the bulk of his book is directed to establishing this source of Baudelaire's psychological vagaries by voluminous citations from the author's works and letters and intimate journals. We may assume that Dr. Laforgue has collected all the available evidence for his thesis (I have not thought it necessary to hunt through the documents for any omission), and with this striking result: there is not a single sentence in all this mass of quotations which justifies his theory. That Baudelaire was in a sense a "mother's boy"; that he was constitutionally as child and man unfitted to face the actualities of life; that he was by instinct and habit driven to seek some escape from the world; and that as child and man he found refuge in the protective love of his mother, and rebelled bitterly when that protection was partly withdrawn by his mother's second marriage—all this is abundantly shown by Dr. Laforgue's documents.

It is clear enough also that Baudelaire was dominated to an abnormal degree by sex, and that the perversions of that domination can be connected with his inability to face the normal realities of life, which, if you choose, you may call an "inferiority complex"; but for the thesis that all this sprang from a sexual attraction as an infant to his mother, for this, I repeat, there is not an iota of evidence. Dr. Laforgue's Freudianism is bare theory with not the slightest basis in known facts; it is pseudo-science in the most blatant form.

And what may be called the accessories of this theory are, if anything, more preposterously fantastical. On page 202 Dr. Laforgue has an explanation of the (supposed) fact that Baudelaire's eye became at the last a veritable sexual organ enabling the artist, as a non-participating spectator, to realize the most extraordinary emotions of man and woman; this he derives from *l'acte sexuel (le coït des parents) auquel il aurait assisté dans son enfance.* To all which common sense can only reply that it is a more than dubious hypothesis to suppose that such an infantile experience would have such an effect, and that it is bare hypothesis, if not ugly disregard of truth, to assume as fact that Baudelaire ever had such an experience. But the climax is reached on pages 164 ff. Here Dr. Laforgue quotes from one of Baudelaire's letters the recollection of a day when he had driven in a fiacre with his mother who had just come from a *maison de santé.* This event the critic interprets quite arbitrarily as referring to the memory *d'une fausse couche ou de quelque chose d'analogue* (note the beautiful ambiguity) *qui l'aurait frappé et intrigué* in his early infancy, and then from this unbased supposition derives the poet's life-long *hantise du sang, de la mort et de la volupté,* and the whole orientation of his tastes.

This, I maintain, is unwarranted conjecture dressed in the imposing garb of pseudo-science, and I believe the unmitigated Freudianism exploited by Dr. Laforgue (his book is of 1931) has been repudiated by the more intelligent psychoanalysts of the present day—if intelligent is not too strong a word. But there is an element of truth in such a theory, which explains why it is still the psychology of the mob, whatever may be the momentary attitude of professional psychologists. No sensible man will deny, or ever has denied, the enormously important factor of sex in the conduct and character of men. So far the Freudian is on safe ground. His error is in deriving this impulse and giving it a peculiar twist from the hypothetical experience of the child in relation to his or her parents. And from this error, which has the plausibility of false simplification dear to the unintelligent, flows a theory rather philosophic or ethical than scientific— the supposition that the sexual impulse as it is formed in the unconscious experience of the child is the basis of nature, and that any conscious inhibition of it is unnatural and consequently deleterious. I shall never forget a Sunday afternoon not many years ago when, marooned in a New York club with a prominent physician, I listened to a series of tales exhibiting the hideous and almost incredible effects of this belief, got of course at second or third hand, among the idle rich women of "Fifth Avenue."

The first step towards a comprehension of Baudelaire and of the literary movement starting from symbolism is to distinguish between the falsehood and
truth of a Dr. Laforgue, and to lay bare the motives
that lie even deeper than sex and are the real springs
of individual and group psychology. Here we have
the assistance of the long line of books by Baron
Ernest Seillière, and particularly, for our purpose, his
study of *Baudelaire,* in which he has analysed and
applied these motives with indefatigable industry.
Seillière, as ought to be well known by this time, finds
two main impulses which have always been at work
in the human soul, but have become prevalent in society since the days of Rousseau. These he designates
as imperialism and mysticism. By the former he means
—what Hobbes long before Rousseau had formulated
from his reading of antiquity—the lust for power,
and ever more power, the *libido dominandi.* But this
common human instinct becomes mystical when reinforced by a belief that the lust of domination is cor-
roborated and sanctified by the ultimate forces shap-
ing our destiny. In its last stage mysticism takes the
form of identifying the soul as an individual entity
with the whole of ultimate reality. The inevitable and
ruinous outcome of such a creed, however unformu-
lated and half-conscious it may remain, is to let loose
the whims or passions of the individual Ego, to dis-
solve the transmitted conventions acquired by the race
from long experience, to relax the inhibiting control
of reason, and to give as it were a divine sanction to
the passing moods and desires of the "soul." With all
this Seillière is careful to distinguish between such
a false exaltation of the individual and the very con-

trary state of Christian mysticism as governed by humility and by a true pessimism born of the conviction of original sin.

In Baron Seillière's schematization this mystical imperialism, or imperial mysticism, falls into a variety of species as one or another mood of the Ego usurps the field. It is naturalistic when the interest in nature leads to identification of the Self with the visible world of phenomena as the ultimate reality; passional when the *libido sentiendi,* particularly in the form of sex, prevails, and the lust of the flesh is decked out with all the radiance of a divine influx, or inspiration; sociological when a special group presumes to speak for society as a whole, and the *volonté générale* is identified with the will of God—"the people can do no wrong"; aesthetic when Beauty, set up as an ideal independent of the True and the Good, opens a field in which the creative imagination is omnipotent with the resulting theory of art for art's sake; metaphysical when the Ego is rationalized as an absolutely autonomous entity.

Now it will be clear that in the realm of modern French poetry, which is our present concern, the last two of these forms of romantic exaltation, the aesthetic and the metaphysical, are of the essence, so to speak, of the movement, and that the other species of mysticism—naturalistic, passional, and sociological— furnish the material employed by the poet in grasping at the sense of power in self-expression. And we can understand why these poets looked to Poe's theory of art as the source, or one of the sources, of aesthetic mysticism, and to Whitman's "barbaric yawp," though less definitely, as an incentive to metaphysical mysticism. But practically, as we see these two guiding principles brought together in the efflorescence of symbolism and *surréalisme,* it is not easy to see which of them is primary and which secondary. In other words, does the poet's conceit of his art, as a product of his pure creativity, lead to a sense of himself as an autonomous entity, or does that metaphysical conception of the self lead to a sense of the autonomy of art? That is a problem not easily solved. Indeed this ambiguity of order inevitably raises the question whether there may not be a single psychological principle which lies behind them both, and of which they are both but different phases. And it seems to me that a closer consideration of the movement we are studying suggests that there is such a principle and that it may be expressed in a single phrase: *the lust of irresponsibility.* Just that, a rebellious hatred of responsibility to any overlordship of law or personal sovereignty, would appear to be the essence of Seillière's imperialism, rather than the lust of dominating others in the Hobbesian sense of the word. And that, equally, would account for the setting-up of art as a field in which the poet can escape the prosaic demands of life. I believe I am right in holding this lust of irresponsibility, which may of course easily pass into the lust of domination, to be one of the primary and universal instincts of human nature, though in most men it is more or less concealed by imbecility of will, or is held in check by the traditional conventions of society. In Mr. C. S. Lewis's wise and witty allegory of modern life, under the title of *The Pilgrim's Regress,* there is a chapter (the sixth of Book VIII) in which this lust of irresponsibility, as I would call it, is expounded

theologically, somewhat in the manner of Francis
Thompson's *Hound of Heaven,* as flight from God
and as the horror of being overtaken by a Being to
whom all the secret impulses of the heart are bare:

All things said one word: CAUGHT—Caught into slavery
again, to walk warily and on sufferance all his days, never to be
alone; never the master of his own soul, to have no privacy, no
corner whereof you could say to the whole universe: This
is my own, here I can do as I please. Under that universal and
inspecting gaze, John cowered like some animal caught up in a
giant's hands and held beneath a magnifying glass.

Mr. Lewis is writing an apologue of the compul-
sory "regress" of a soul back to the Law-Giver from
whom it had fled for liberty; but the revolt of his hero
is not unlike the Hindu's horror of the impersonal
law of Karma.

What I find then in Baudelaire, and my finding is
amply confirmed by the masterly study of Baron Seillière, is exactly such a passion of autonomy. Most
clearly and directly this shows itself in his tenacious
grasp of Poe's theory of pure art, and somewhat less
clearly, though not less directly, in his exaltation of
the artist, *i.e.,* himself, in face of the restrictions and
decencies of bourgeois convention as personified for
him in his stepfather. All this is coloured and clouded
no doubt by abnormal sexuality; but the lust of irresponsibility, I would maintain, is primary. The only
means of attaining such a liberation is through valiant
denial of any supernatural reality which can hold
him to judgement. And the consequence—for the soul
of man, to adapt the words of St. Augustine, is un-
quiet until it finds rest in some ultimate reality—the
consequence is that, having repudiated any authority
from above the plane of conventional human nature

he will grope for some reality below that plane. What lends a peculiar note to Baudelaire's poetry and distinguishes it from the types that follow is the fact that, however fiercely he may protest against it in language, emotionally he is unable to throw off the feeling of responsibility. This substratum of nature, this dark abyss of the irrational subconscious out of which emerges the stream of fantastic images and perverted desires, is the reality, but in the shadow of the supernatural, defied yet never obliterated from his conscience, it is the devil's kingdom of *evil*. Hence the poet's homage to its dark power will take the form of diabolism, and in his soul the spirit of revolt will retain some parody of the Christian hue of sin under the masque of blasphemy. These are not fancies : his diabolism and blasphemy are the romantic substitute for acknowledged responsibility; they give to Baudelaire's tortured imagination a note of orthodoxy that connects him, in his despite one might say, with the great and serious tradition of art. Beside him the poets of the succeeding generation appear as triflers or at the best as naughty children.

For what one sees in the course from symbolism to *surréalisme,* through all the sporadic reactions which in fact only make the main line of development more pronounced, is the Baudelairian lust of liberation divesting itself of any remnant of the hated responsibility to the supernatural and revelling in the irresponsibility of the infranatural, with less and less sense of evil connected with this lower reality and indeed, in its more characteristic moments, with no distinction between good and evil. The recognized philosopher of the movement is Paul Valéry. In his lucid

pages, if anywhere, *le prestige d'être soi* rises to the
aerial heights of a metaphysical finality. The proper
aim of the intelligent man (*l'homme de l'esprit*) is to
distinguish himself from everything which in *le moi* is
not pure consciousness. What is a thought or a specific sentiment but a sensation prolonged? What is any
felt desire, what are all the phenomena of the inner
life, in the sight of *l'esprit,* but intrusions into consciousness from the outer world? things which are
born and die, suffer change, are substituted one for
the other, to the Ego an unmeaning flux from which
pure mind must separate itself by a process of con-
tinual exhaustion? So it is that to attain to absolute
consciousness of self the obligation arises to detach
one's self from nature and life, to deny responsibility
to anything whatsoever. And so it is that at the end of
this intellectual asceticism the *moi pur* as it were
moults itself into a nameless power, a cosmic point in
the vast vacuity; or, as M. Valéry expresses it, the
man of intelligence (*l'homme de l'esprit*) must at the
last reduce himself scientifically to be nothing whatsoever.

That is the ideal. But what of the world outside of
pure contentless consciousness, with its insistent at-
tacks and appeals? In spite of his spiritual metaphysic
the poet is a man tenderly attached to his soul and
body, drawn by them like Narcissus leaning over the
water, tempted by this life so strange and incomprehensible, by these adorable colours thrown by life
over the sunset of consciousness, and coming one
knows not whence; still he is seduced by the illusion
of living and takes pleasure in the seduction, though
not without regret for the ideal of absolute disdain

and perfect vacuity—such is the poet, and so M. Valéry appears to us. In the end "nothing exists save two distinct presences, two incommensurable natures; there are only two adversaries who watch each other and do not understand," states of being—or of non-being? one knows not which. In such a split and self-destructive universe the soul will fight for its existence by its own pure creativity through the instrument of words. "The world of poetry is essentially closed and complete in itself, being purely the system of the ornaments and accidents of language." So the soul, drawing back from the annihilation of pure egotism, will build about itself a world of its own out of hints and shreds of actuality. At any price it has escaped responsibility.

Something of this ideal of pure poesy is common to all the writers for whom Valéry speaks as the recognized philosopher; and it is fair to say that at times they do evoke a strange haunting beauty caught in the irrational enchantment of words. But these children of symbolism were men as well as poets, and could not escape their destiny; their boasted freedom, deep down in their hearts, they know to be a sham. It is not a joyous band, these singers of irresponsibility —I speak of those in the main line of advance, not of those on the outskirts, and obviously not of those whose only relation to the movement is one of opposition. Beneath the exultations of license and the frivolities of conceit, he who listens can hear, deep down, the rumbling note of doubt and defeat and despair.

Finally I would like to quote again from Mr. C. S. Lewis. In the nineteenth volume of *Essays and Studies by Members of the English Association,* he has a paper on *The Personal Heresy in Criticism* all of which bears on the problem I have been discussing. It closes with this paragraph:

Surely the dilemma is plain. Either there is significance in the whole process of things as well as in human activity, or there is no significance in human activity itself. It is an idle dream, at once cowardly and arrogant, that we can withdraw the human soul, as a mere epiphenomenon, from a universe of idiotic force, and yet hope, after that, to find for her some *faubourg* where she can keep a mock court in exile. You cannot have it both ways. If the world is meaningless, then so are we; if we mean something, we do not mean alone. Embrace either alternative, and you are free of the personal heresy.

RELIGION AND SOCIAL DISCONTENT

[An address delivered at Lake Forest College in 1921 at the inauguration of President Herbert McComb Moore. Reprinted by permission from the Bross Library, Vol. XI.]

A COUPLE of years ago one of the most distinguished of our social philosophers, Professor John Dewey, of Columbia University, was invited to lecture at the Imperial University of Japan, and, having delivered his message in Tokyo, proceeded to China, where he was welcomed eagerly by the younger malcontents as an exponent of Western ideas. The character of these ideas which our collegiate missioner carried across the Pacific Ocean may be learned from the little book since published by him under the title of *Reconstruction in Philosophy*. His thesis, indeed, is simple almost to naïveté. Hitherto, he avers, philosophy and religion have been nothing but an attempt to "identify truth with authoritative dogma." And this attempt has a double aspect, theoretical and practical. On the one hand, mankind is prone to forget the evils of yesterday and to gloat in memory over the good, so that by the combined force of memory and imagination the past remains with us as a kind of idealized dream, a lovely, impalpable curtain hanging between our vision and the hard realities of the present. From such an iridescent dream has grown the philosophical and religious belief in an immaterial world of ideas, a glamorous make-believe under whose sway "we squirm," as Mr. Dewey says in his pragmatic style, "dodge, evade, disguise, cover up, find excuses and palliations—anything to render the mental scene less uncongenial," and so to escape the actualities that confront us. Buddha, Plato, Jesus, and the other great masters and doctors of the life unseen were merely juggling with words and leading us nowhere; the discipline of character proposed by them and their offers of supernatural peace were a fraudulent perversion of the facts of human experience. The only true knowledge is that which comes to the farmer toiling at his crops, and to the carpenter labouring with his tools; the real facts of life are those that we can see and smell and taste and handle, and, so far as I can understand Mr. Dewey, such things alone.

That is the theoretical aspect of the reconstruction of philosophy proposed by our tender-hearted materialist; and the practical aspect is like unto it. Existing forms of government, established order, property, the church, institutions generally, draw their support from the idealizing illusions of memory and imagination; they are in truth the dead hand of the past clutching the throat of the living present. Throughout all the ages preceding the advent of Mr. Dewey, or by a gracious inclusion anterior to Francis Bacon, it has been the task of philosophers and religious leaders to find reasons for the existence of such institutions on ideal grounds, and to justify those who profit from them at the expense of the masses. Religion and philosophy have been simply the servile allies of the predatory classes of society. The hope of the world is in the new gospel of pragmatic materialism.

I trust I have not misrepresented Mr. Dewey's

teaching. Indeed, with an individual teacher I should
have no quarrel, were he not in a position of authority; but it is another matter when such doctrines are
spreading out from a lecture-room all over the country, and, as I hear from Chinese friends, are persuading the young reformers of the Far East that the only
salvation for their people lies in adopting the crudest
materialism of Western civilization, and in emanci-
pating themselves from all that philosophy and religion hitherto have meant to the Occident as well as to
the Orient. At least here is a matter to consider.

Now in one sense Mr. Dewey's theory of religion—
I use this word preferably, since the classical forms of
philosophy which he would reconstruct belonged essentially to the field of religion—in one sense this
theory is so far from being revolutionary that it has
been current almost from the inception of human
thought. Plato knew that the religious temper was
naturally reverential of the past and conservative in
its influence. It was, indeed, for this reason that he
gave to religion and to a philosophy of the unseen
world so thorough a control over the polity of his
state. Polybius, the Greek historian of Rome, not only
recognized this function of religion, but went so far
as to maintain that even the palpable fictions of superstition should be upheld as a safeguard against political anarchy. "Since the multitude," he argues, "is
ever fickle and capricious, full of lawless passions, and
irrational and violent resentments, there is no way
left to keep them in order but the terrors of future
punishment, and all the pompous circumstance that
attends such kinds of fictions. On which account the
ancients acted, in my opinion, with great judgement

and penetration, when they contrived to bring in these notions of the gods and of a future state into the popular belief." And on this basis Polybius goes on to show how the power and permanence of Rome were connected with a national morality grounded in irrational beliefs, whereas the inquisitive rationalism of Greece was the cause of her ethical and political decline. Livy's annals of Rome are inspired throughout by the same idea, though without the tincture of scepticism that pervades the philosophy of the Greek historian. The city on the Tiber, Livy thought, grew mighty and conquered the world because of her faith in the gods and in that mystical Fatum which presided over her destiny and kept her, through all the formal changes of her government, true to her original *êthos*. "You will find," he writes, "all things have prospered for those who follow the gods, while adversity dogs those who spurn them—*invenietis omnia prospera evenisse sequentibus deos, adversa spernentibus*." So, for Tacitus, religion was, as he expresses it in his epigrammatic way, *instrumentum regni*. Christianity, though it altered much, maintained this same view. The greatest preacher of the ancient church, Chrysostom, was fond of pointing to the connection of religious humility, mother of all the virtues, with the principle of orderly subordination, on which, as on the golden chain of divine law, depended the stability of society and the happiness of the people.

But I must not fatigue you with examples. Passing on to the eighteenth century, one finds the politico-religious thought of England and France dominated by the Polybian notion that religion was imposed

more or less deliberately on the people by their masters
as an instrument of government, only with this important difference, that in England the imposition was
commonly regarded even by the more radical deists
and freethinkers as a salutary and necessary fraud,
whereas across the channel a more logical and less
prudential habit of speech led the bolder spirits at
least to spurn the whole fabric of traditional religion
as an impediment to liberty and progress. Bolingbroke, atheist or deist, as you choose to call him,
would take the position frankly that the truths of
scepticism are for the enlightened few who, as Aristotle said, have learned from philosophy to do voluntarily what other men do under compulsion. Religion,
to Bolingbroke and his class, was simply an integral
part of that marvellous fiction, the British Constitution. "To make a government effectual to all the good
purposes of it," he says, "there must be a religion;
this religion must be national, and this national religion must be maintained in reputation and reverence." And a little later in the century one of the
correspondents of that admirable and very British
gentleman, Sir William Pepys, condemns Gibbon for
divulging to the public the sort of scepticism which
he might have enjoyed lawfully in his closet. "I
agree," avows our correspondent, "that no man
should 'take the bridle out of the mouth of that wild
Beast Man' (as Bolingbroke writes to Swift). . . .
Tho' a man may be allowed to keep poisons in his
closet, he shall not be permitted to vend them as
cordials." Nothing is more characteristic of the ruling
temper of England than the fact that this same Gibbon, he who had expended his wit and his vast erudi-

tion in "sapping a solemn creed with solemn sneer," in his old age should have confessed admiration for Burke's chivalry, even for his "superstition," and should have planned a dialogue of the dead, wherein Lucian and Erasmus and Voltaire were to be heard discussing the danger of shaking the ancient faith of the people in religious institutions.

But the French mind could not rest in this severance of logic and practice. To their more incisive and less humble way of thinking, true was true and false was false, and to confound the boundaries of truth and falsehood was only to pay homage to canting hypocrisy. There was no distinction for them between an illusion and a plain lie, nor would they rest satisfied with a suppression of truth as known to individual reason, in order to leave room for a practical faith as taught by public experience. So it happened that the *philosophes* as a body were not theoretical sceptics merely but militant atheists. If, as La Mettrie believed, "the soul is an empty word of which no one has any idea," if men are no more than blind "moles creeping in the field of nature," then, o' God's name, out with the truth of it; society can only profit from universal knowledge of the facts. In like manner a Holbach will take up the old theory of Polybius, but without the Polybian and the British "reserve." "Experience," he says, "teaches us that sacred opinions were the real source of the evils of human beings. Ignorance of natural causes created gods for them. Imposture made these gods terrible. This idea hindered the progress of reason." And again: "An atheist . . . is a man who destroys chimeras harmful to the human race, in order to lead men back to nature, to experience, and to reason, which has no need of recourse to ideal powers to explain the operations of nature."

And the French view has prevailed, or threatens to prevail, as courageous views inevitably tend to supplant timid views, however true it may be that courage in such matters may sometimes be another name for insensibility, not to say conceit. So Leslie Stephen, writing of the eighteenth century in England, with a sneer that contrives to combine the French boldness with the British reserve, declares that "the church, in short, was excellent as a national refrigerating machine; but no cultivated person could believe in its doctrines." And at last Mr. Dewey, perhaps the most influential teacher today in America,[1] is renewing the old cry and persuading our young men that religion is a fallacy of the reason devised to maintain the more fortunate classes in their iniquitous claims, and that progress and democracy are bound up with the materialistic pragmatism that emanates from his own chair of reconstructed philosophy.

Now, it will be clear from these illustrations, which might be multiplied indefinitely, that the classic philosophy, the philosophy of idealism properly so called, which underlies all religion, whether Platonic or Christian, has been regarded by most thinking men from ancient times to the present day as a conservative, or at least as a regulative, force in society. But thinking men have differed profoundly in their valuation of such a force. Those who hold this philosophy

[1] I doubt if this is quite true now. Since the Russian revolution the issues have been sharpened, and the sentimentalism of the older materialists has been discredited.—Note added to present edition.

to be true are naturally undivided in their opinion that its social function is beneficial; but those sceptically and materialistically inclined, to whom the spiritual world of Plato and St. Augustine is merely an insubstantial fabric wrought out of the discontent of mankind with the actualities of life, have been divided in their attitude. By some this dream of the unseen, though a deception, has been accepted as necessary for the ordered welfare of society; the enlightened few might indulge their superiority of doubt, but without the restraining content born of superstition the turbulent desires of the masses would throw the world into anarchy and barbarism and universal misery. That was the prevalent attitude of ancient rationalism; and it is still common enough today among those who have a condescending respect for the Church as a useful ally of the police court. To others, a rapidly growing number, it seems that the spirit of content engendered by religion, if based on a falsehood, must be detrimental to the progress of mankind. Or perhaps their position might be expressed more accurately by reversing the terms. They would not say that religious content is false and therefore must be detrimental; but, rather, religious content is inimical to progress and therefore must be false.

I am not for the moment concerned to examine the truth or falsehood of the ideal philosophy which supports religious institutions; that is a question which for the present we may waive. We will not discriminate between those who hold this philosophy to be true and those who regard it as an illusion, but an illusion necessary for the preservation of society. The line for us is drawn between those who, for whatever reason, cling to a religious philosophy of the unseen and those who denounce such a philosophy as a check to the progress and prosperity of the race. And you will see at once that the issue between these two classes has been sharpened for us of the present day by the intrusion into sociology of a new theory of existence —new at least in its scope and claims. I mean the great and all-devouring doctrine of evolution.

Now the evolutionary philosophy, by which we have become accustomed, rather prematurely perhaps, to test all problems of truth and utility, has many aspects and follows various lines of argument. What it means to the working scientist is one thing, and what it means to the metaphysician may be quite another thing; but when it intrudes into the field of sociology, and more specifically when it lays its grasping hand upon that part of sociology which attempts to weigh the value of religious belief, you will find it almost inevitably taking the note so clearly defined in pages of Mr. Dewey's typical book. Evolution is identified with progress, progress is measured by increased power to satisfy physical wants, and the effort to increase this power is conditioned on dissatisfaction with material conditions. Oh, I know that many evolutionary sociologists will demur against the reduction of their theories to a crudely materialistic formula; but many of them will not, and I am sure the formula does not misrepresent the real conclusions of their doctrine. It comes down to this: Physical progress has its source in physical discontent, and, by an extension of terms, social progress has its source in social discontent; and any doctrine which dulls the edge of this discontent is thereby an obstacle in the

path of individual and racial welfare. Discontent is
motion and the striving for better things, it is life;
content is just stagnation and death. And here lies the
charge against religion. By drawing off the mind to
the contemplation of those so-called eternal things
that are not visible to the bodily eyes or palpable to
these fleshly hands, by injecting spiritual values into
this present life and raising hopes of other-worldly
happiness, religion, together with the whole range of
illusory philosophy on which it is nurtured, throws the
feelings of physical discomfort out of the centre into
the further margin of the field of vision, into the
penumbra, so to speak, of insignificance, while it im-
poses a stillness of content upon the naturally restless
soul of man. In such a mood the past, out of which
the oracles of faith seem to sound by some miracle of
memory, acquires a tender sanctity, and the institutions of tradition are often invested with a reverence
and awe which easily flow into vested rights. If the
religious mood were really to prevail, they say, then
society would sink into the slothful decay described
by old Mandeville in his *Fable of the Bees,* that
terrible poem which the modern humanitarian would
abhor as a black parody of his doctrine, but which in
good sooth told the facts of a materialistic sociology
once for all:

> All Arts and Crafts neglected lie;
> Content, the Bane of Industry,
> Makes 'em admire their homely Store,
> And neither seek nor covet more.

What shall be said of these contrasted views? I
think first of all we must say that the issue is confused
by an ambiguity lurking in the terms employed. And
this is no new thing. It is, in fact, one of the curiosi-

ties of our human warfare that the most bitter dis-
putes on the most fundamental questions often go
round about in a circle because the two parties to the
dispute do not see that the same word may be used in
different senses. So it is certainly of content and discontent; and a man's attitude may very well be determined by his understanding or misunderstanding of
the double meaning of these words. Cardinal Newman, perhaps the keenest psychological analyst of the
past century, has insisted on this distinction in one
of his sermons:

> To be out of conceit with our lot in life is no high feeling—it
> is discontent or ambition; but to be out of conceit with the ordi-
> nary way of *viewing* our lot, with the ordinary thoughts and
> feelings of mankind is nothing but to be a Christian. This is the
> difference between worldly ambition and heavenly. It is a
> heavenly ambition which prompts us to soar above the vulgar
> and ordinary *motives* and *tastes* of the world, the while we abide
> *in* our calling; like our Saviour who, though the Son of God and
> partaking of His Father's fulness, yet all His youth long was
> obedient to His earthly parents, and learned a humble trade. But
> it is a sordid, narrow, miserable ambition to attempt to *leave*
> our earthly lot; to be wearied or ashamed of what we are, to
> hanker after greatness of station, or novelty of life. However,
> the multitude of men go neither in the one way nor the other;
> they neither have the high ambition nor the low ambition.

If that sounds oversubtle, or if the preacher's as-
sumptions seem to beg the question, let us drop the
pulpit jargon and look at the distinction as it works
out practically in the lives of two highly useful members of society, the plumber and the college president.
Suppose a plumber is called into your house on a raw
day of January to tinker up a disordered pipe in the
cellar. Probably that plumber is discontented; indeed,
I cannot imagine how a plumber can be anything but
discontented. Nevertheless, his discontent may be

either one of two very different sorts. He may be grumbling to himself because he has to work at a cold and dirty job, while you are enjoying your newspaper upstairs over a warm and cosy fire. In that case his discontent may take itself out in slighting his task and wasting your time and lengthening his bill. These things are said to happen. And he may even carry his discontent into a view of the organization of society which expresses itself in very hardy politics. But suppose now that his discontent takes another form. Imagine him content with his lot as a plumber, even proud of it, but dissatisfied with the common reproach of slackness and extortion, ambitious to excel in his profession. I do not cite such a plumber as a probability; but all things are possible in a Bross lecture. At any rate, such a paragon would be worthy of succeeding to that famous chair of the Harvard faculty once occupied by a gentleman whom the trustees hired as the Plummer professor of Christianity, but whom the undergraduates irreverently dubbed the Christian professor of plumbing.

And so the other end of the scale, the college president. He too is said sometimes to be discontented; and again his discontent may assume either one of two forms. He may be ambitious of size and *réclame* for his institution, and may measure his dignity by the number of students over whom he presides. His alumni are likely to encourage him in this, and I have myself known the head of an ancient university in the East who used to scan the catalogues of the great Western institutions year by year with bitter jealousy and heart-burning as their register of students gradually approached his own, and then shot beyond it.

Inevitably such discontent leads to a lowering of standards, mitigated by the pious belief that that form of education is noblest which is desired by, and accessible to, the largest number of paying candidates. Thus a debasement of education becomes identified in his mind with social service. But one can imagine another kind of discontent, which should pursue just the opposite course. Its standard would be qualitative, not quantitative, and it would fear the temptation of size not the murmurs of ambitious alumni. It would look for its reward not in a swelling registration or spreading houses or additional courses of study, but to its success in attracting the better minds and the stronger characters and in directing these in the narrow and tried paths.

However it may be with the plumber and the college president, clearly these words, content and discontent, are replete with ambiguity; they are consequences rather than motives of conduct, and we cannot safely argue upon them until we have looked more closely into the springs of action which control respectively the religious and the natural life. And here I must beg you to indulge me in a bit of pedantry. Our English speech, with all its practical efficiency, has never developed a very precise ethical terminology, and so to get at the distinction I have in mind I am going to ask you to consider two rather outlandish-sounding Greek words which were much in use among the early moralists of our era. One of them is *tapeinophrosynê*, the other is *pleonexia*.

Tapeinophrosynê is a compound word, meaning primarily lowness of mind; it embraces the idea of humility and meekness, but neither of these conveys

its full significance. St. Paul uses it in the Epistle to
the Ephesians, where it is translated specifically "lowliness," but its force really runs through the whole
passage: "I therefore, the prisoner of the Lord, be-
seech you that ye walk worthy of the vocation where-
with ye are called, with all lowliness (*tapeinophrosynê*) and meekness, with long-suffering, forbearing
one another in love; endeavouring to keep the unity
of the Spirit in the bond of peace." Paul had in mind
the saying of Christ recorded in the Gospel of Matthew, where an equivalent phrase is rendered "lowly
in heart": "Come unto me, all ye that labour and are
heavy laden, and I will give you rest. Take my yoke
upon you, and learn of me; for I am meek and lowly
in heart: and ye shall find rest unto your souls." And
the first of the Beatitudes contains the same idea in
slightly different language: "Blessed are the poor in
spirit (*i.e.,* the lowly in heart), for theirs is the kingdom of heaven." This, then, is the virtue, or, rather,
as Chrysostom calls it, the mother of the virtues, which
was upheld by the fathers, without exception one
might almost say, as the basis of Christian character
and the motive of religious living—*tapeinophrosynê*.
And the result of such a virtue, as it works itself out
through character into content and discontent, is readily seen. It lays the axe at the very root of that restlessness, that uneasy ambition, that natural instinct
of jealousy, that covetousness forbidden in the Tenth
Commandment. It goes even further than that. You
may have observed that the blessing bestowed in Matthew on the "poor in spirit," in Luke is directed simply to the "poor," or "beggars," as the word might be
translated. Now Luke, it is fair to say, introduced a

disturbing element into religion by his habit of giving
this materialistic turn to spiritual graces. But it remains true, nevertheless, that this glorification—the
word is scarcely too strong—of poverty, or at least
of the freedom from material possessions, as in itself
a state of blessedness, is a note not only of all the
Gospels but of most of the other great religious books
that have moved the world. Always Chrysostom, to
refer again to the model Christian preacher, connects
humility with the twin virtue of charity. And charity,
as he commends it, is not so much an act of giving
out of sympathy for the sufferings of the needy and
downtrodden—though this feeling is not absent—as
it is a voluntary act of surrendering our worldly possessions in the belief that in themselves they may be
a snare to the spirit. For Chrysostom, in a very literal
sense of the word, it was more blessed to give than to
receive. If religion suffered discontent to abide in the
heart of a man, it would not be because he owned too
few of this world's goods, or felt humiliated by his
relative rank in society, but because the world was too
much for him. For true content he should look to
treasures laid up elsewhere and to riches that the eye
of the flesh could not count.

So much for the religious motive of humility. *Pleonexia,* the driving force of the natural man, might be
defined as its exact opposite. Etymologically, as an
ethical term, *pleonexia* means simply the reaching out
to grasp ever more and more, whether this impulse
show itself in the grosser appetite for possessions, or
in the ambition to overtop others in rank and honours,
or in that universal craving which Hobbes regarded

as the state of nature: "A general inclination of all mankind, a perpetual and restless desire of power after power, that ceaseth only in death." To call this the natural state of man might seem to involve a libel against both nature and man, but by natural, as you see, is meant only the condition of mankind if all those restraints were excluded which we have defined as religious. And such a liberty has never lacked its advocates as being not only the natural but the rational, even the ideal rule of conduct. It would be easy to prove this by abundant citations from modern writers; indeed, the name of Nietzsche leaps to one's lips; but as I have already trespassed on your patience by the introduction of Greek terms into my definitions, I will presume further by going for my illustrations to the people who coined the expression. In one of the dialogues of Plato, then, you may hear a respectable citizen of Athens rebuking Socrates for his fantastic notions of conduct, and arguing for what was really the popular code of morality:

The makers of laws are the many weak; and they make laws and distribute praises and censures with a view to themselves and to their own interests; and they terrify the mightier sort of men, and those who are able to get the better of them, in order that they may not get the better of them; and they say that dishonesty is shameful and unjust; meaning, when they speak of injustice, the desire to have more (*pleon echein*) than their neighbors, for knowing their own inferiority they are only too glad of equality. . . . I plainly assert that he who would truly live ought to allow his desires to wax to the uttermost, and not to chastise them; but when they have grown to their greatest he should have courage and intelligence to minister to them and to satisfy all his longings. And this I affirm to be natural justice and nobility. But the many cannot do so; and, therefore, they blame such persons, because they are ashamed of their own inability, which they desire to conceal, and hence they say that intemperance is base.

This is manifestly the Hobbian view of the natural state of man, thought out long before Hobbes, not to mention the naturalists of our own day. And it was not theory only, but practice. Turn to Thucydides' *History of the Peloponnesian War,* which Hobbes translated, and from which, though this is not generally known, Hobbes borrowed the principles that stirred up the seventeenth century as Nietzsche troubled the nineteenth. Read there the famous debate between the envoys of Athens and the magistrates of Melos. The Athenians are advising the Melians, whose racial affinity was with Sparta, to submit their city to the empire of Athens; and to the Melians' argument from justice they reply with cold-blooded candour:

"We tell you this, that we are here now both to enlarge our own dominions and also to confer about the saving of your city. . . ." "But will you not accept?" plead the Melians, "that we remain quiet, and be your friends (whereas before we were your enemies), and take part with neither." "No," reply the Athenians, "for your enmity doth not so much hurt us as your friendship would be an argument of our weakness, and your hatred of our power, amongst those whom we bear rule over. . . . As for the favour of the gods, we expect to have it as well as you; for we neither do nor require anything contrary to what mankind hath decreed either concerning the worship of the gods or concerning themselves. For of the gods we think according to the common opinion; and of men that for certain, by necessity of nature, they will everywhere reign over such as they be too strong for. Neither did we make this law, nor are we the first that use it made, but as we found it, and shall leave it to posterity forever, so also we use it."

Such was the philosophy of the natural man in ancient Greece, and such is the philosophy of the natural man today, however it may be disguised and glossed over; it is based on the instinctive motive of *pleonexia,* the "perpetual and restless desire of power after power, that ceaseth only in death." I need not dwell on the kind of discontent it begets in the soul, a discontent intrinsically and totally opposite to that which accompanies the purely religious motive.

But you will say that these principles of conduct and the feelings that go with them are mere abstractions, fictions of the analytical reason; no man is, or can be, purely religious as I have defined the term, or purely naturalistic. And that is true, is in fact the point at which I am aiming. On the one hand, no man can utterly uproot the natural impulses out of his soul; and if a few men in a generation approach anywhere near it, the saints and martyrs and lonely sages, they are by their virtues cut off from the common life of mankind. Were all men, or even a considerable proportion of men, at any time to overcome the natural discontent that drives us on to seek greater possessions and higher honours and more power, then, surely, all ambition and invention would die, the wheels of progress would slacken and stop, civilization would fail, and society would sink back into barbarism, so far at least as we measure civilization and barbarism by physical standards. Such would be the issue of "content, the bane of industry."

On the other hand, it will be said, and by none more loudly than by the champions of sentimental naturalism who belong to Mr. Dewey's school, that the picture of the man controlled by the "perpetual and restless desire of power," and by that alone, is a pure caricature of human nature. Even a Napoleon, they will say, who might stand for the model of such a monstrosity, yet had thought for the glory of his land, and was a great reformer of laws and institutions. So, too, the Athenian envoys in Thucydides, cynical as

were their confessions of the desire of power to rule
their own people and all peoples, nevertheless were
compelled to mix some honey in their gall, and tried
to persuade the Melians that the hegemony of Athens
would be prudently exercised and would promote the
well-being of her subject states.

Such an objection we readily grant. It is perfectly
true that the creature in whom the instinct of greed
and the lust of power should reign without modifica-
tion or mitigation would be no man at all, but a rav-
ening beast of prey. Both the religious man and the
natural man, as I have portrayed them, are avowedly
abstractions, at least to the extent that no society
could exist if composed of either type in its purity.
They are abstractions, but they are made such by ab-
stracting one of the two contrasted impulses that do
reign together in virtually every human breast, and
by showing what would result if one of these impulses
were so allowed an unhampered sway over a man's
conduct. And now and then, in some rare individual,
the one or the other of these types has been realized
almost in its purity, the religious type in a St. Francis
of Assisi, with his ideals of poverty and chastity and
obedience, the natural type, if not in a Napoleon or an
Alexander, yet in certain notorious criminals who
have raged through life with the ferocity of a starv-
ing wolf.

The truth we must recognize is that both these
motives exist in the human heart, and that the conduct of man, not as the saint would see him in the
cloister nor as the evolutionist would see him in the
jungle, but as we see him in the market-place and the
theatre and the courts and the home—that the conduct

of man is a resultant from these two contrary impulsions.

Now, it is fair to say that religion has always recognized the legitimacy of another standard of life besides the one peculiarly its own. It has seen clearly that the ideal of poverty and chastity and obedience, which would uproot altogether the natural instincts, is possible for very few men, and that the attempt to enforce such a standard absolutely on society at large would result in a world of hypocrisies, if it did not actually run counter to the command of the Creator. So the Christian Church, even in its most ascetic days, admitted that property and marriage and prestige were the normal condition of life; and Buddhism drew up two distinct tables of law, one for the religious state pure and simple, the other for the mass of mankind who are engaged in practical affairs. But both Christianity and Buddhism held that the natural instincts were ruinous if left to themselves, and that they became salutary instruments of welfare only when limited and softened and illuminated by a law not of themselves.

On the contrary, it is of the very essence of naturalism that it should admit no standard but its own. To a naturalist and materialist of the true type all the ideal philosophy of the past, with the religion which grows out of it, is a lying cheat of the imagination and corresponds to nothing real in the nature of things; its peace is a pitiful sham cherished by those who are too cowardly to face the facts; its promise to mitigate the harsher passions of greed is only a cunning pretext devised to blind the dispossessed of their rights and to fortify the owners of wealth and power in the unmolested enjoyment of their criminal advantages. From the very beginning the double standard of things spiritual and material has been the foe of progress, and only then will justice and peace and prosperity prevail, when the deceptions of priest and philosopher are swept away and our vision of material values, as known to the scientist in his laboratory and to the blacksmith at his forge, is not confused by false lights. This, I repeat, is no caricature of the sort of naturalistic pragmatism that is sweeping over the world.

I would not imply that all these enemies of religion, or even those of them who are most influential today, are conscious advocates of a pitiless egotism or believe that the repudiation of religion would throw mankind into that anarchy of internecine warfare which Hobbes described as the state of nature, or which Nietzsche glorified as the battle-field of the superman. It is rather the mark of modern naturalism that it is plastered up and down, swathed and swaddled, masked and disguised, with sentimentalisms. A Dewey, for instance, wields his influence over the young and troubled minds of our generation because he stands forth as a reformer with a precious panacea for the calamities of history. It is the dream of another realm, such reformers declare, that has riveted upon us the chains of lethargy and despair; shatter these, let men become aware of their real nature, let them see that the only truth is to recognize this life as all they have, and that their only hope of happiness is to get together and increase the physical comforts of existence—let this once come to pass, and at last a peace born of universal benevolence will settle down upon this long-vexed planet. Sympathy, they maintain, is a natural instinct of the heart, as surely as the lust of power and possessions; rather, it is the genuine basis of nature, and of itself will control the other natural instincts if unhampered by false ideals. That is a pretty faith; but is it true? No doubt the human heart is swayed by sympathy and benevolence; but are these the qualities of the natural man? I will not go into the answer given to this question by the religious minds from Plato down to Cardinal Newman, who all with one accord assert that sympathy and benevolence of an active sort do not spring up from the soil of nature, but result from the reaching down, so to speak, of a higher principle into the lusts of the flesh. They all maintain, with one voice, that the only effective bond of union, whether it be of friendship or of society, is through our perception of oneness in the spirit. Mercy droppeth down as a gentle dew from heaven. I will not argue from this thesis, because it would carry us into the brier patch of metaphysics. But history and science both would seem to enforce the bitter conviction that at the best the instinct of natural sympathy is a fragile and treacherous support against the assaults of a restless and perpetual desire of power. Greece learnt this, to her frightful ruin, when she followed the law of nature as avowed by the Athenians at Melos; and today we have rediscovered it in the same desolation of war. That, I fear, is the lesson of history. And science has no different lesson. Indeed, by the natural man I would signify precisely the realization, if such were possible, of the principle of natural selection and the survival of the fittest by which the world is governed as the scientist, the natural philosopher, as he used to be called, sees it when he eliminates the religious idea from his view. I mean nothing more than what Huxley, the protagonist of evolutionary philosophy, meant when, in his essay on *The Struggle for Existence,* he thus described the law of nature as actually seen in operation:

> From the point of view of the moralist, the animal world is on about the same level as a gladiator's show. The creatures are fairly well treated, and set to fight—whereby the strongest, the swiftest, and the cunningest live to fight another day. The spectator has no need to turn his thumbs down, as no quarter is given. He must admit that the skill and training displayed are wonderful. But he must shut his eyes if he would not see that more or less enduring suffering is the meed of both vanquished and victor. And since the great game is going on in every corner of the world, thousands of times a minute; since, were our ears sharp enough, we need not descend to the gates of hell to hear
> *sospiri, pianti, ed alti guai,*
>
> *Voci alte e fioche, e suon di man con elle.*

And I think, if you look closely into the social theory based on the naturalistic, or let us say the purely economic, view of life, you will find that beneath its mask of sentimental sympathy the reality is a face of greed and animal rapacity. According to this theory, progress is a result of discontent. Because men are discontented with their present state they push out for something better. And no doubt in a half-way that is true. But when discontent is associated with material standards alone, and purchasable comfort, and worldly opportunity, or, to put the matter in its most favourable light, when success and the goal of achievement are measured by the pleasures, however you may refine them, and by the pride of a few brief years of physical existence, beyond which there is nothing, and when for failure in these no compensation is held out, no supernatural hope, no refuge of peace, here and now, such as the world cannot give—when the driving force of progress is so presented, what is there in the nature of things to offer in the long run any effective resistance to the innate desire of power after power that ends only with death? What equal counterpoise will you set against that instinct of *pleonexia* which reaches out for ever more and more?

Philosophy is full of mockeries. These honourable gentlemen who are teaching a pure naturalism in the schoolroom, who denounce the content of religion and other-worldly philosophy as a base acquiescence, who in the restlessness of an itching egotism go out as missionaries to the people of the far Orient, may deceive themselves and may try to deceive us; their language may be sleek with the sentiment of brotherly love, but strip off its disguise, and the social theory they are proclaiming will leer forth in its true face as an incentive not to progress but to the anarchy of the jungle. These men are distilling into society a discontent that knows no satisfaction, that must engender only bitterness of disappointment and mutual distrust and hatred, and that in the end, if not checked by other motives, will bring about internecine warfare and a suicide of civilization of which the hideous years through which we have just passed are a warning admonition. And these teachers have the field today. We applaud them for their pretensions of philanthrophy, even when we doubt the utility of their philosophy. We are browbeaten by the volume of their noisy propaganda. We are mealy-mouthed and afraid to speak out in open denunciation, even when secretly we burn with indignation at the baseness of their words. We sulk in silence, as if we had nothing to say. Meanwhile they have had the field to themselves, and the world every day is more filled with fear and disquiet.

There is no danger that by opposing other views of life to this insolent naturalism we shall put an end to that normal discontent with material conditions which may be a necessary incentive to natural and social progress. Certainly, however it may have been at other times, we need apprehend no such danger now. In a world manifestly distracted and blown from its moorings, in a society seething already with envy, it is not the part of wisdom to sow broadcast words that are calculated to inflame discontent into passionate hatred or sullen despair. That way leads to madness. What we need is rather a clearer perception of, and a firmer insistence on, those immaterial values which it is within the power of every man to make his own, whatever may be the seeming injustice of his material condition. We need rather to emphasize the simple truth that poverty is not the only, or indeed the worst, of mortal evils, that happiness does not consist mainly in the things which money can buy, that the man of narrow means may enrich himself with treasures which only he can give to himself, and which no one can take from him, that the purest satisfaction is in the sense of work honestly done and duties well met, and a mind and conscience at ease with itself. Even to the very poor, if such must be, religion may offer manifold compensations. "Blessed be ye poor," it was said, "for yours is the kingdom of God." Shall we say that these words were spoken in ignorance or jest or mockery? I think not. We for the moment may have lost the key to their meaning, we may have listened to teachers who turn them into ridicule; nevertheless, they are true words, rich with a gift of solid content.

But it is not the less fortunate and the poor alone, or I might even say chiefly, who need to hear the precepts which the new philosophy is drowning with its clamorous tongue. If the home of theoretical materialism is in the lecture-rooms of philosophy, the home of practical materialism is in the offices of Wall Street. If there is any truth that needs to be reiterated today, it is the simple truth that a man may heap up riches and increase his power indefinitely, and command all the visible sources of pleasure, and still be a poor, mean creature, a mere beggar in the veritable joys and honours of life. He that has many possessions needs be a strong man to escape their strangling grip. They wrap him about, they colour all his thinking, they hang like a heavy curtain, as if were, between himself and his soul. You have heard the saying: "It is easier for a camel to go through a needle's eye than for a rich man to enter into the kingdom of God"; that is a hard lesson, but in reality it is only an Oriental way of expressing what Plato had taught long before in the Academy: "Neither when one has his heart set on gaining money, save by fair means, or even is at ease with such gaining, does he then bestow gifts of honour upon his soul; rather, he degrades it thereby, selling what is precious and fair in the soul at the price of a little gold, whereas all the gold on the earth and under the earth is not equal in value to virtue." That is the invariable lesson of religion and the idealistic philosophy. Certainly, it is a truth we shall not recover by listening to the words of the new naturalism. It is not by a philosophy that preaches social discontent as the means of progress, and measures content by material values, however it may disguise the banality of its aims in a sentimental philanthropy—it is not by such a philosophy that justice and mercy and humility shall be imposed upon the natural pride of those who have the larger share of this world's goods.

It is true that religion, or religious philosophy, as its friends and foes have seen from the beginning, is an alleviator of discontent and a brake upon innovation; but the content it offers from the world of immaterial values is a necessary counterpoise to the mutual envy and materialistic greed of the natural man, and the conservatism it inculcates is not the ally of sullen and predatory privilege but of orderly amelioration.

CHURCH AND POLITICS

[Delivered as an address at the Commencement Exercises of the General Theological Seminary, New York, May 1934; published in the *American Review* for September 1934]

MR. DEAN, Right Reverend and Reverend Sirs, ladies and gentlemen, I feel very humble in this presence, knowing that I ought to be among the listeners rather than standing here as speaker. And you of the graduating class, who are about to set forth upon your delicate mission as priests of the Church, and to whom in particular I am engaged to speak—if I were an orator trained to elicit the goodwill of an audience, I should be congratulating you on your successes in the school and flattering you with suave prophecies of the noble work you are prepared to accomplish. Above all my address should abound in glorifications of the venerable institution which you serve, lauding it as a guardian of the pure faith and as the guide of a world distraught by religious doubts. But I am not at all an orator; only a plain man, one troubled by much that I see going on about me, and ill at ease at what seems to be the direction the Church is taking to meet the turmoil of the age. And so I am venturing to assume the rôle of critic, though fully aware of the absence of any claim to such a title, and fearful that, under the necessity of being brief, my words may imply a dogmatic assurance which I am far from feeling.

Two or three weeks ago I heard a sermon preached by the agent of the General Council of the Church in the field of social relations, and as such possessing a certain note of authority. It was an eloquent address, and manifestly was well received by the congregation. More than that, its doctrine seemed to me to fall in with what I am hearing from other pulpits and with what I am continually reading in books and magazines of an ecclesiastical stamp. It recalled to my mind the conversation of young priests I have known, filled with the zeal of their orders to remake the world. It brought up before me the grandiose gesture of the Archbishop of York, than whom no one stands higher in the Church, when recently through the pulpits of his diocese he raised a thousand voices to instruct, if not to intimidate, the British Government in its disposal of the income from taxation. It seemed to me as I listened that I was hearing the authentic voice of the Church, at least of that faction of the Anglican Church in America which today is most keenly alive to its sacred duties. I was carried along with the rest of the congregation; yet all the while another small voice within me was asking whether we were not dreaming of a fools' paradise in place of the Kingdom of God.

Religion, I heard, and hear, has two functions, (1) the salvation of the individual soul and (2) the redemption of society. To that doctrine no one I suppose would object. Nor would any one take exception to an argument designed to show in what wise the Christian character of the individual should manifest itself so as to contribute to the Christianizing of society. Of the need for social reorganization in these days of unrest and fear and cruel unemployment there can be no doubt. It is the means chosen for the achievement of this reformation and the nature of the reformation to be achieved that worry me in so much that I hear, and leave me often wondering whether I am listening to a sermon or to a political harangue. For the goal set in view it is fair to say that, so far as I know, only a small minority of the priesthood would be ready to identify the activity and influence of the Church openly with any one form of government, whether it be a transformed feudalism or capitalism or fascism or out-and-out Marxism. Nevertheless the burden of the arguments I hear is political to this extent that their trend is towards what might be called a sort of sentimental socialism. I may be misrepresenting the special sermon to which I have referred, but I am not wrong, I believe, in holding that a vague ideal of equalitarian brotherhood, to be introduced by an equally vague humanitarian sympathy, has been very widely accepted by the Church as a modern equivalent for what Christ meant by the Kingdom of God and repentance.

Now in so far as such an ideal is only a disguise for a specific ordering of society, it is a pure illusion. If there ever was a party of practical socialists who held that an equalitarian state could be established and maintained on the sentimental love of man for man, it certainly does not exist now; it was a dream very quickly extinguished by the stern lessons of history. Will you find warrant for such a faith in the economic fatalism of Karl Marx? Will you discover it in the theory of the Soviet rulers of Russia, who to the determinism of Marx have added the conscious will to power of the proletariat? If the Church thinks she can join the tide that seems for the moment to be sweeping the world towards communism, and at the same time believes an injection of soft sentiment can so control that movement as to overcome its naked materialistic and anti-religious tenets, then indeed the Church is indulging in hopes of a fools' paradise. The socialists know better; they are wiser in their own generation than the so-called children of light; they understand that they must govern by the discipline of force and not by appeals to the heart.

And this law holds good not only in relation to socialism but for any other form of government; it holds because of the bitter fact that wherever sentiment comes into open conflict with the innate egotism of mankind and the innate will to power, sentiment simply shrivels up as a motive of conduct. It is too often forgotten that the same Adam Smith who, in *The Wealth of Nations,* formulated the law of competitive industrialism, was also the author of *The Theory of Moral Sentiments.* On the one hand, according to the economic treatise the greed of individuals aiming each at his own enrichment would by the bare result of competition and *laisser-faire* balance out in general welfare and content. On the other hand, the apparent barbarity of so mechanical a system is humanized by the moral sentiment of sympathy which causes a man to suffer involuntarily with another in calamity or to rejoice with another in prosperity, and which checks any overweening impulse of greed and dominion by participation in the feeling of resentment aroused in the victim of injustice.

It might seem as if this balance of natural selfishness and natural sympathy would act as a substitute for the ethical dualism expressed in the Platonic and Biblical psychology of a warfare within our members, with the need that a man's first duty is to be master of himself. And it is true that the counterplay of natural instincts did, and does, simulate the working of the classical ethics. But to a very limited degree, and only in a few outstanding characters. In the main Adam Smith's combination of *laisser-faire* with moral sentiments, as it was put into practice by the succeeding age, resulted in that competitive industrialism which came to a climax in the so-called Manchester school of economics, and from which the world today is swinging towards an equally hard-bitten communism. Nor is the reason for this difficult to detect if we follow out Adam Smith's acute analysis of the operation of the law of natural sympathy.

"It is not," Smith declares, "the love of our neighbour, it is not the love of mankind, which upon many occasions prompts us to the practice of those divine virtues [that is, the virtues of justice and unselfishness]. It is a stronger love, a more powerful affection, which generally takes place upon such occasions; the love of what is honourable and noble, of the grandeur and dignity and superiority of our own characters." That would seem to be setting morality on a very different basis from bare instinctive sympathy. But mark the sequel. This love of the honourable and noble turns out to be no more than a sense of our own superiority, a bit of vanity, and our vanity turns out to be only a reflex of sympathy by which we feel for ourselves the indignation felt by those who might suffer from our rapacity. And very characteristically the operation of this sympathy is to keep the poor in their place and to render the rich secure in their possessions. "The poor man," our moralist continues, "must neither defraud nor steal from the rich, though the acquisition might be much more beneficial to the one than the loss could be hurtful to the other. The man within immediately calls to him in this case, too, that he is no better than his neighbour, and that by his unjust preference he renders himself the proper object of the contempt and indignation of mankind, as well as of the punishment which that contempt and indignation must naturally dispose them to inflict." In other words the moral sentiment of sympathy, when put to the test, becomes a mere veneer upon the law of absolute self-interest. What we really have is a philosophy that unchains the natural instincts of men and believes that out of the conflicts of such impulses progress evolves by a sort of mechanical determinism.

Now I am not supposing that any churchmen of today will admit the approximation of his ethics to the sentimental naturalism of Adam Smith. He will asseverate that the sentiment he advocates as a check upon the wolfish appetites of mankind has its source in the supernatural and comes to him through the grace of God; and that the brotherhood of Christianity calls for a reversal of Adam Smith's order by placing the obligation of self-control primarily upon the rich rather than upon the poor. But is the distinction as sharp really as the churchman deems it? Oh, I know there is a difference. The Church cannot forget the first and great commandment which

directs us to the love of God, and cannot, even with
the best endeavour, hide the fact that the second
commandment, though like unto the first, is subsidi-
ary to it. I know that our pulpits and our pious literature resound with exhortations to the pure love of
God. That is well, no doubt; it is a true element of
religion. And yet—if you will bear with my rude and
perhaps crude comment—when, hearing these sermons, I look about at the congregation, including
myself, and when, reading these books of piety, I try
to calculate their probable effect upon others like
myself, then depressing doubts creep upon me; I
cannot away with them. After all, what does the love
of God mean to the average man in the pew? If I
may judge from myself, nay, if I can judge from
what I see and hear, it is to us for the most part a
beautiful phrase, and only at rare intervals anything
more solid than that. And—dare I ask?—does it
often mean anything quite clear and definite and
dynamic to the priest who repeats the phrase as a
kind of acquired and holy habit?

Such questions are audacious, and may proclaim
nothing more than my own incompetence as a critic
of religion. But when it comes to the love of one's
neighbour, I dare speak with more assurance. It does
not sound a hollow phrase, this second commandment, on the lips of the preacher; it does not fall
without genuine, often exciting, effect upon the ears
of the listener. But I note this curious and disconcerting fact. Commonly in practice—not always, not constantly, but commonly in practice—the pleading for
brotherly love gains in vividness and clarity and di-
rectness and sometimes in passionate urgency, just

in proportion as the pleading for love to Godward
becomes vague in outline and muddy in texture, while
perhaps conventionally exaggerated in expression. I
do not say that this should be so; indeed it should
not be so. But I assert it as a fact within my experience; and it all leads on to the horrid insistent question, whether this sentimental socialism, which
threatens to become official with the Church, does
not spring from depletion rather than from surplus of
faith, whether its fervour for economic change does
not imply a dullness towards things of the spirit,
whether the love to which it appeals, despite the traditional language of theology sometimes, though now
not very often, draped about it, is in substance much
more than the instinctive sympathy of Adam Smith
and the naturalists intensified to the fanaticism of
religion.

This is not to imply that the sentiment of Christian
love is purely illusory and futile. That sentiment does
in persons of rare gifts bear beautiful and precious
fruit; it may even have some effect in mitigating the
cruelties of social life. So the naturalistic sentiment
of sympathy showed itself here and there in sweeten-
ing the characters of men caught in the hard industrialism of the Manchester school of economics. But
by and large neither the sentimental love of the Christian nor the sentimental sympathy of the avowed
naturalist, left to itself, can be trusted when brought
into rivalry with the naturalistic impulses of greed
and expansion and the naturalistic will to power. History proves too clearly that the feeling for others,
whether religious or naturalistic, in general simply
crumples up at the touch of the feeling for self when

the more unruly passions are aroused. The capitalistic society of today is our witness, and the lords of the Russian communism have learned the truth which the sentimental socialists of the Church are refusing to face. Lenin understood that the success of revolution depends on capitalizing, so to speak, the individual's will to power as the will of a particular class.

What then shall we say? Must religion forgo any purpose to save society and must it limit itself to the salvation of a few exceptional persons, "the world forgetting, by the world forgot"? And even so, how is the individual soul to be reached? I remember the righteous indignation with which a young priest once turned upon me with the question, for him a very practical problem, how he could bring any thought of religion to a man distracted with the anxieties of unemployment, or how he could talk to a man of his soul's welfare while the body was unfed. Well, is it impertinent to quote the words of Christ in the wilderness after he had fasted forty days and the devil bade him turn the stones into bread? Certainly Christ did not confuse religion with food or think it should be deferred until the hunger of the body was satisfied. Hunger is an evil, no doubt; it should be alleviated. But hunger is not the only evil of life, or the most devastating. There are pains of the flesh more agonizing than starvation; there are calamities more terrible than social injustice. And what is your religion worth unless it can bring healing to the broken-hearted and to the downtrodden a hope not of this world? What a mockery is made of the gospel if it cannot be preached to a man until the iniquities of society have been set right. Is that the spirit of the beatitudes? The call of religion is first of all and last of all to a soul conscious of its own guilt, the function of religion is first of all and last of all to offer to a soul despairing of this world's peace the promise of eternal life. When under the shadow of an atrocious death Christ said to his disciples: "These things I have spoken unto you, that in me ye might have peace: in the world ye shall have tribulation; but be of good cheer, I have overcome the world,"—when he uttered these words, perhaps of all the words that fell from his lips the most wonderful, he was not announcing a gospel of economic regeneration or postponing the hope of peace until the wrongs of capitalism should be overcome, nor was he identifying the moral obligations of the individual soul with a sentimental socialism. If you care to know the logical outcome of involving religion in a social programme, read the *Reflections on the End of an Era* recently published by Reinhold Niebuhr. In that brilliant and startling and at the last fatalistic and totally irreligious book, this is the conclusion you will hear: for the moral man of today the only choice is "between hypocrisy and vengeance," the hypocrisy of a moralized industrialism and the vengeance of a moralized communism.

Is then—the question is insistent—the only mission of Christianity to rescue a few wrecks from the outrageous seas of worldliness? has it no help for the community? To this extent it has none, that to immerse the Church in politics, whether it be of a feudalistic or capitalistic or fascist or communistic type, is to abandon the Kingdom of Heaven for a utopian mockery. To this extent, that to identify the driving force of religion with an outgoing sentiment of love is to leave mankind a prey to the unsentimental forces of nature.

Religion, I insist, is concerned primarily with the individual soul, and in that concern must now and always reckon with the fact that, whatever the organization of society may be, sorrows there will be in this earthly existence, and above all other causes of sorrow the sting of transitoriness and the tragedy of death; and religion must now and always reckon with the terrible fact of sin. I am not inferring that the concern of religion for the individual may not, and should not, have its repercussion in the relations of man to man. My doubt of the dominant attitude of the Church in these matters is that she tends to mistake the goal and to rely on insufficient means. This everlasting note of sentimental socialism, however it be named or left unnamed, seems to indicate that the Church has set her heart on the creation of an equalitarian brotherhood as the Christian opposed to the pagan ideal of society. But equalitarianism is an impossible ideal for the simple reason that men are not, and will not be, the same, and that they are not equal. Certainly if the history of the last twenty years has taught anything, it is that mankind is not capable of self-government. The communist as well as the fascist or the monarchist has learnt that an efficient organization cannot be erected on an equalitarian basis. They know that men are divided roughly into three main groups: the mass of those who must be externally controlled by fear or by blind obedience; a ruling body, whether an individual or a committee, which holds the reins and drives, ostensibly at least, for the good of the whole; and an intermediary class who voluntarily submit to direction and upon whose allegiance to the principles embodied in the actual government the stability of the State depends. And equalitarianism, even were it practicable, is an unethical ideal, because it slurs over the fact of human depravity and so weakens the moral sense by attributing all the ills of life to society and none to the individual sufferer. It is in line with this shifting of emphasis that I hear so much about the rights of man and virtually never a word about his personal responsibility. Justice demands a more equal balance between the two.

And the idea of brotherhood, though praiseworthy in itself, seems to me, as it is actually advocated, to imply a reliance on inadequate means. Whatever the ultimate, or temporary, form of government towards which we are drifting, surely the contribution of Christianity should be to moderate the natural passions of men, to chain the innate will to power, to check the expansive lust of possession, and to make the right prevail in place of sheer might. But this precisely is what the principle of sympathy alone will not do. Against the egotism of the natural man that motive, unsupported by a stronger appeal to the spirit, will leave society defenceless against the inhuman determinism of an Adam Smith or a Karl Marx.

If this were all, the Church would be in a bad way, and there would be some excuse for the growing indifference of the secular mind to religion as a pretty but feckless annex, if not a malignant obstacle, to the fatalistic operation of economic laws. But it is not all. Sympathy and love are good in themselves; they are sentimental when they fail to take account of what from the beginning and everywhere, not only in Christianity but in all the great religions, has been the real stay of the spirit in its competition with the lusts of the flesh. It was not the love of God or of man by itself that started the Church upon its victorious course. Preponderantly it was the preaching of the imminent Kingdom of Heaven that united the little band of disciples about their Lord, and that Kingdom was conceived vividly in terms of the supernatural; it was in essence not sociological but eschatological. The preaching of Jesus began with the terrifying threat: *Repent, for the kingdom of heaven is at hand*; it closed with the sublime assumption: *I am, and ye shall see the Son of man sitting on the right hand of power, and coming in the clouds of heaven.*

The early community of Christians was dominated by this belief, and we can see exactly how, as the parousia was deferred decade by decade and the expected catastrophe did not occur, the hope and fear of the imminent kingdom gave way to the thought of an otherworldly heaven and hell and of judgement to come after death. The driving force of religion remained eschatological; only the scene and the time were changed. And so the idea passed on through the dark centuries to the Middle Ages and beyond. The great commandment was not forgotten. The uncompelled love of God mastered the souls of a few of the mystics so deeply that they were in spirit rapt from the world; the love of man inspired some of the saints

to heroic devotions of self-sacrifice. But for society at
large, for the ordinary believers, the love of God was
intimately, and wholesomely, mingled with fear; it
was God the Judge before whom they bowed in
trembling awe, and His sentences were the eternity of
heaven and the eternity of hell. If you have any doubt
of this, recall the pictures of the Last Day, or read
the extracts from the sermons of the Middle Ages in
Dr. Owst's huge collection. Not the sentiment of love,
not appeals to sympathy, but a lively imaginative
grasp of spiritual values made the Church a power to
mitigate, if she could not eradicate, the egotistical
passions of men and to give some cohesion to society.
And still, if you think this a passing phase of the
Christian faith at a dark period of its history, then
turn to your Lucretius and learn from him how hopes
and fears of the future life haunted the mind of pagan
antiquity; or study the annals of a greater religion
than that of Greece and see how for the Buddhist the
otherworldly judgements of Karma gave sanction to
the precepts of morality, while the endless weariness
of transmigration drove the more sensitive souls to
longing for the peace of Nirvana.

And unless the Church of today can recapture some
of that realization of spiritual values her preaching
of love to God will fall on ever deafer ears, and her
pleas for the brotherhood of man will evaporate into
a sigh or do a little to hasten the advent of an anti-
religious State governed by those who understand
human nature better than she. I do not say that even
so the Church will convert the world to a community
of saints or install that sentimental socialism for

which she is yearning; human nature will not be altered to that extent, nor have we any warrant in scripture or history or psychology to suppose that sin with its hideous consequences will disappear. But of this I am convinced, that the one effective weapon of the Church in her campaign against the unnecessary evils of society, her one available instrument for bringing into play some measure of true justice as distinct from the ruthless law of competition and from the equally ruthless will to power of the proletariat, is through the restoration in the individual human soul of a sense of responsibility extending beyond the grave. I am aware of the difficulties attached to such a programme. The mediaeval realism of heaven and hell, with their physical delights and tortures as we see them portrayed in a Dante, has gone; and we would not return to it, if we could. But some equivalent for the hopes and fears connected with such an eschatology we must discover. We must reawaken the minds of men to the fact that this earthly existence is only a small segment of everlasting life, that its significance lies hidden in the long reaches of the future, that somehow the results of what we do here and now will pursue the soul in her flight through eternity with a train of blessings or curses, that salvation and damnation are not empty words but awful possibilities fraught with infinities of peace or despair. How that shall be accomplished, how these spiritual truths are to be reclothed in the garments of the imagination and made persuasive to the conscience it is not for me to say; that will be the task of you who are going out into the world as authoritative spokesmen of the Church. Only so much I would conjecture, that the path to such a reformation lies through a sounder conception and a broader expansion of the Catholic doctrine of the sacramental nature of life.

A SCHOLAR-SAINT

[Published in the *American Review* for March 1935]

URING his life Baron von Hügel, to those who knew him intimately and could appreciate him, was perhaps the outstanding impersonation of religion in England, a man combining the most alert sensitiveness to the philosophical problems of theology with the most unquestioning zeal of Christian faith. There was about him the mystery of a splendour flaming from a hidden source, something at once attractive and unapproachable. Mr. Edwyn Bevan, a fellow member with him of the London Society for the Study of Religion, so described him: "Those who heard the Baron speak at one of these meetings will never forget it—the grey hair standing up from his forehead, the large dark eyes in a face as of fine ivory, the divine fire which seemed to fill him, the passionate sense of the reality of God, which broke forth in volcanic utterance, strange bits of slang and colloquialisms mingling with magnificent phrases, and left him, when ended, exhausted and trembling." And to another member of the same society, Claude Montefiori, he was, more simply, "the great scholar-saint."[1] There are signs today that his influence is broadening out; but his ever-searching philosophy needs, for quicker comprehension, to be ordered and organized, and such a task Mr. A. Hazard Dakin,

[1] Quoted by Bernard Holland in his Introduction to the *Selected Letters*, pp. 35 and 36.

Jr., has undertaken and, on the whole, admirably executed in his study of *Von Hügel and the Supernatural,* recently published. If the following briefer essay at interpretation closes on a note of adverse criticism, I trust this will not be laid to lack of reverence for one whom, though known to me only through his writings, I accept and would extol as indeed a scholar-saint.

The father of our subject was an Austrian and a Baron of the Holy Roman Empire, distinguished in his day as a traveller, an antiquary, and a diplomat. In 1852 he was Minister to the Grand Ducal Court of Tuscany, and at Florence in that year his son Friedrich was born. The mother was a Scottish lady, so that the boy was bilingual from birth. In 1860 the Baron was transferred to Brussels, where he remained for seven years. Here Friedrich got most of his education (he was never at school or university), and added French to his English, German, and Italian. In all these languages he corresponded freely, and he had besides an adequate knowledge of Latin and Greek. Later the family moved to England and settled at Torquay. The father died in 1870. Three years after that the son married Lady Mary Herbert, sister of the thirteenth Earl of Pembroke. Their home was finally in London, and there, in 1925, our Baron ended his life.

As gradually von Hügel became better known he received frequent invitations to lecture. To these calls he responded as far as health permitted, and we have seen the impression he made on the group of notable men who met together in London for the discussion of religious topics. He published also several books, of which I take *The Mystical Element of Religion* and the two volumes of *Essays and Addresses* to be the most important. He was a laborious writer, to whom language seemed rather an enemy to be overcome than a friend of the spirit; and it must be confessed that he is often laborious to read. Adjective is piled upon adjective, strange abstract substantives are coined, parenthetical clauses are tangled together; his periods occasionally fall into awkward involution as if he were thinking in another tongue and translating his thoughts literally for the printed page, and indeed he says somewhere that seven-tenths of his reading was done in German. Yet withal he was a great writer, and, if style is the man, a great stylist. At times his sentences, even whole paragraphs, have the epigrammatic perfection which comes when a thought or image has been held in the mind until, beaten free of encumbrances, it stands out in naked simplicity. Even his clumsier pages have the merit of transcription; beneath the clash of Teutonic and English idiom it is as if we heard the very voice of a great spirit in travail.

For saint and scholar though he was, one cannot read his *Letters* (which in my estimation have a value beyond that of his writings for the public, just because they bring us closer to the man himself) without feeling that here was a soul wrestling with some interior obstacle which kept his ideas and emotions from coalescing in final harmony. There is depth of emotional experience and there is breadth of thought, but in the end not the equipoise of mind that philosophy can impart, nor the measure of peace beyond understanding that religion ought to confer.

No doubt his deafness enforced a certain isolation from general society for which he was not responsible; but beyond that there breaks out now and then through the communications with his most intimate friends a cry of loneliness which is of the soul and not of circumstance. To Miss Petre, who was suffering "more or less of a nervous breakdown," he writes: "So I can sympathize, even from my own immediate feelings, but far more, of course, because of the many *years* of my life, when I was, I am sure, far worse than you can be." Loneliness and nerves, these are not the dominant note of his *Letters,* and it was the example of high heroism that drew to him the more spiritually minded of his contemporaries; but perturbation was there also, a cloud of unclarity never entirely dispersed.

Anyone familiar with von Hügel's works will have been struck by the recurrence of two words, "tension" and "costingness," which seem to be the best terms he could find for the focal points where all his thinking and all his deeper emotions converge.

By tension he means something primarily very simple and quite universal—the bare fact that every man, even the least introspective, feels himself drawn in two directions, that there is a certain duality of ends inherent in his nature as a human being. However immersed he may be in the pursuit of business or pleasure, there will come to him moments of revulsion when he longs for an inner repose and self-realization not given by the distractions of daily life. With reflection and deepening experience this polarity of attraction becomes a more permanent factor of consciousness and a more sharply defined division of obligations. It has passed under the sway of religion, and shows itself in the feeling that somehow we are related to two divergent spheres, and that somehow a double demand is laid upon us to make ourselves right with this world and with what, in distinction, we call the other-world. To the Christian this final polarity of experience appears, objectively, in the contrast between Creator and creature, and, subjectively, in the alternations between attachment and detachment as these range all the way from the humblest needs of the body, through the larger interests of reason and imagination, up to the practice of religion in worship and prayer and adoration.

Now this tension of the inner life, as I have said, is in varying degrees common to all men and is the distinctive mark of humanity. The degree may be very low. It may be true of most men that they feel attachment and detachment rather as passing moods than as a settled state; they drift from moment to moment, from interest to interest; and if by reason of greater vehemence of will or passion they become strongly attached to the successes of this world, the sense of detachment is correspondingly lessened to flickering instants of doubt. But with von Hügel we cannot read even a few of his pages without recognizing that here was one to whom both worlds were powerfully and coincidentally present, whose interest in both was vividly real, and the whole set of whose will was to live in both by comprehension rather than by alternation. Hence the polarity, which ordinarily produces only a fluttering from side to side, is felt by him as a constant problem of consciousness in the answer to which lies the measure of the fullness of life. Hence too the response of the reader, the feeling that here is a true man, in comparison with whom most others, by reason of their one-sided development, seem but embryos of humanity, mere potentialities rather than actualities, which "slip from our grasp like a shadow or a dream."

His love of family, particularly of his oldest daughter, was a passion in which we see brought together the instincts of nature and the implication of soul with soul in the longing for an eternity of common worship. His friendships were wide and strong, rooted at once in human attachment and in mutuality of spiritual help. His interest in science and secular philosophy, to a less extent in art and literature, was close and genuine. At the same time one is struck by the effort to discover in all these fields a contribution to religion, where perhaps in themselves they might seem to be pulling in the contrary direction. This is especially true of his attitude towards Victorian science, as may be seen in his frequent elevation of Darwin into a model for Christian disinterestedness, and in his readiness to turn theories of materialistic determination into a lesson of Christian humility before the vast reach of spiritual law. Intellectually he is broad almost to the point of failing to admit certain final incompatibilities; if there is weakness here, it is not of narrowness or prejudice, but in some lack of indignation. A friend of his has noted that the only things over which he was wont to be indignant were Christian Science and Mrs. Besant.

And this conscious contrast at once and drawing-together of the two ways continues on into the formalities of religion itself. Now the doubling of appeal is between the immediacy of the inner light and the mediation of sacramental grace, between the privacy of a soul with God and the commonalty of worship. Through all his life the Baron was drawn to the mystics, with their tendency to substitute personal ecstasy for the mediatorial office of the Church, and his own spirit of devotion was so intensely individualistic as to leave him never quite at ease with the authoritarian policy of Rome; yet on the other side no one could speak more eloquently of the advantages of institutionalism or submit more humbly to the great tradition. Nothing is more characteristic of the man than the accounts of the wide-sweeping independence of his conversation with a friend, during a walk into the country, and then of his rapt, child-like adoration before the Host in some barren little church as they were nearing home.

All this is not only the figure of the Baron's life, but makes the constant burden of his philosophy. Perhaps the most explicit and complete of his many attempts to define his position occurs in *The Mystical Element of Religion,* Volume II, page 127; but, as briefer and as illustrative also of his indebtedness to a certain group of Germans, I take this passage quoted by him with approval from Troeltsch:

This multiplicity [of moral ends] can be further determined as the contrast between two poles, both imbedded within man's nature, from which proceed the two chief types of ends, the religious and the this-worldly. It is the polarity of religious and of humane morality, neither of which can be missed without moral damage, yet which, all the same, refuse to be brought to a common formula. Upon this polarity reposes the richness of our life, and also its difficulty; but from it also there ever arises anew the ardent endeavour to find some unification.

These might be the words of the Baron himself. And from the "difficulty" involved in this polarity and from the need of "ardent endeavour," one is carried immediately from his insistence on tension to the other great term of his vocabulary, "costingness." Here again the idea is borrowed from one of the simplest and most universal phases of human experience. It needs no philosopher to teach us that every good thing in the market of this world must be purchased at a price. He who will win out in any of the affairs of life must pay for his success, whether it be in business or the professions or politics or learning or art, in the self-enlargement of marriage and friendship or the mere possession of one's self in peace. That is the law of compensation from which there is no escape, least of all in that footing between this-world and the other-world which is the way of religion. Here is the place where tension and costingness, as the Baron knew, come together at their highest point.

Now the cost of religion may show itself in either one of two exactions. It may demand the breaking of all ties to the things of this world, even to those in themselves most innocent and beautiful. This is the way of asceticism, and it is the actual, though never quite frankly acknowledged, ideal of the Roman Church. Or it may exact the sacrifice of ease for such a strenuous unremitting control of temperamental impulse towards either pole of tension as is needed for mediation and adjustment. This is the way of humanism, and it is essentially, I believe, the Anglican ideal of the *via media,* though many of that communion would deny it. Superficially the ascetic may appear to be paying more heavily for his religion

than the humanist; but if one weighs the price in
terms of energy of the will, I suspect that the balance
is on the other side. To give up this world unreserv-
edly for the other, to abandon attachment to all creatures for the single-minded love of God, is costly indeed; but in the end I doubt if it is as hard an act of
faith as that of one who resolves to live in both worlds
at once, rendering to each its proper due, and to love
the creature *as creature* without allowing such an
attachment to detach him from love of the Creator.
Is the religion of the ascetic really purer than that
of the humanist? Is it unfair to ask whether in fact
the ascetic's surrender of this world, if probed to the
bottom, may not be found to harbour a lurking suspicion of surrender to his own unbalanced temper? Is
the renunciation of a hermit like St. Anthony or are
the austerities of a frightened libertine like the Trap-
pist de Rancé higher in spiritual grace, more profoundly Christian, closer to the perfection of a being
who presumedly was placed in this world for a purpose, than the life of a Hooker or a Bishop Ken?

That is a question to which the Baron's Church has
never given an answer quite free of ambiguity. But
of the Baron himself we may assert that, however
vehemently his heart was set on the naked values of
the other-world, he saw and professed that the path
to that goal was through comprehension and mediation. Whatever may have been his attraction to the
great mystics of the faith and to the devotees of
asceticism, his stand on sober reflection was rather
this side of the extreme and towards the humanistic
mean of adjustment.

The very things we, men, are to love and seek [he writes] are also the same things which we are to be detached from, and from which we are to flee. Attachment and cultivation, and detachment and renouncement, will thus each gain and keep a splendid spaciousness of occasions and materials. There will be no fanaticism, but a profound earnestness; there will be no worldliness, but an immense variety of interest and expansion towards all things in their specific kinds and degrees of goodness, truth, and beauty.

He saw clearly, perhaps the more clearly for a certain strain in his own nature, that only by such a balance can the wholesomeness of the spiritual life be kept unimpaired: "It is a difficult art to prevent religion from overstraining us and from thus leading to a very dangerous reaction against itself."

And this art of religion, to be fabricated out of the whole substance of human experience, corresponds with the epistemology, or scientific theory of knowledge, which the Baron accepted under the name of critical realism. Our perception of physical objects, he believed, is evoked by some emanation from them to us, and is thus realistic in the sense that we are in contact with the actual nature of the objective world. At the same time something subjective, some process of our own mind, enters into the act of perception, so that the reality of the object perceived can be known only by a critical analysis of the method of knowing, which can approach but never attain complete objectivity. In similar fashion our knowledge of God starts with the spiritual perception of a presence objectively real, but is conditioned also by the mechanism of our intuitive faculty. Here too clarity depends on the power of separating what is objective from what is subjective. But in this case the critical process is complicated by the fact that from its first beginning the

intuition of God is bound up with the perception of
physical phenomena, and that growth in religion
comes through the whole range of experience, emotional, imaginative, and rational. We can never wholly
abstract our sense of the reality of God from our
relation to the world of physical realities.

All this is in line with the humanistic approach to
the mysteries of religion. Yet the final impression
left in the mind by von Hügel's works is not of pure
humanism. His philosophy presents another aspect
which, at the least, is not easily reconciled with critical
realism, and which I can only explain as a foreign
intrusion from the rationalizing metaphysics of Aristotle and St. Thomas Aquinas and Kant, and to a
lesser degree of Plotinus and Spinoza. This turn of
his thought has to do with the duality of God and
the world, and is primarily a matter of purely intellectual theory, but it works down almost impercepti-
bly, inevitably, into the tensions of actual experience.
As humanist he will say: "What God is in Himself
we, strictly speaking, do not know; all our true knowledge of Him is limited to what He is to us and in
us." As a metaphysician he will define the essence
of Godhead in terms of infinity which, however disguised by negations, does pretend to a positive knowledge beyond what He is to us and in us.

In this field of speculation von Hügel reasons from
the axiom that we must conceive God either as immanent or as transcendent. Now the complete imma-
nence of God, whether in the form of frank pantheism or of Hegelian dialectic, he rejects always, unhesitatingly, and in his later years almost fanatically.
It was this chiefly that caused him to break finally

with his friend Loisy, after following the French scholar's modernism to the verge, if not beyond it, of what in Rome was denounced for heresy. The reason for his antipathy he states in a letter to Father Tyrrell, who was slowly moving in the direction of Loisy, but with whom he remained in friendly intercourse to the tragic end. "If," he writes, "one were to take your clear-cut Immanentism as final and complete, the noblest half of the religious experience of tip-toe expectation, of unfulfilled aspiration, of sense of a Divine Life, of which our own but touches the outskirts, would have no place." There he was speaking from his heart, out of a conviction which no theorem of abstract reasoning could overshadow or confuse or cause to waver. And his words, to the humanist, indeed to the genuine theist, are the charter of religion.

Von Hügel never faltered in his hostility to any form of pure immanentism and in his assertion of the transcendence of God. But there are two ways of understanding transcendentalism, and here he was not so clear or so consistent. To the religious sense as involved in worship and adoration and prayer, and, I should add, to any true philosophy, God is conceived as apart from and above the world, yet still connected with the world and consequently in some manner conditioned by the world. On the other hand, to metaphysics, to religion subjected to the demands of pure reason, God becomes an abstraction totally detached from the world and absolutely unconditioned. Now in what I should regard as his normal state the Baron is strong for the first of these two conceptions; and he defines his position by declaring that God must be both transcendent and immanent. He is sensitively aware of the fact that what faith instinctively looks up to is a divine Personality working in and upon the world as the Agent of teleology, the Creator of beauty and joy, the Judge also, and that to stop there is not obscurantism but humility. Only such a view is in harmony with his constant insistence on the approach to truth through the whole round of experience, and not through "a violent clarifying of the rich obscurities of life" under the tyranny of reason. He is fully aware of the danger of crossing this humbler approach to truth with the presumptions of metaphysical finality. "The touching troubledness of spirit," he says of Plotinus, is "caused in great part, not simply by the greatness of the Reality which he is attempting to seize and express, but by the contradiction between his spiritual experiences and his system's exigencies—between the immensely rich, intensely concrete God . . . and the unpicturable Poverty and Abstractness of his system."

The Baron sees, at his clearer moments, that the error of the "system" is central to the whole metaphysical tradition carried down from Aristotle to the present day, and he can utter sharp criticism of St. Thomas and Kant. He can lay his finger on the root of the false growth of modern German Idealism in Descartes's "fundamental principle" of starting "not from the concrete fact, viz., a mind thinking *something*, . . . but from that pure abstraction—thinking, or thought, or a thinking of a thought." Nevertheless his own indoctrination in philosophy through scholastic and modern German Idealism is too strong for him; he cannot escape the net of their abstractions.

"The thirst of religion is, at bottom," he avows, "a metaphysical thirst, and the intimations of religion are, ultimately, metaphysical intimations." And he knows perfectly well what is implied by this submission to metaphysics. It means, as he states categorically, that God shall be defined in terms of Aristotle's "Unmoving *energeia*," of St. Thomas's *Ipsum Esse,* and of Kant's "Idea of the Unconditioned."

A new tension is thus forced into the centre of religion by this double conception of transcendentalism, as thought rests now in a God associated with, and therefore in some sense conditioned by, the world, and turns now to a God totally abstracted from the world. Which is the God of worship, or are there in fact two Gods? Von Hügel is too honest and too clear-sighted to pass over this difficulty, and his efforts to reconcile the two horns of the dilemma are instructive, and—shall I say it?—to one of his admirers a little saddening. God Himself is absolute, but He wills to be conditioned. "When we say we believe in the Creation, . . . we profess the mysterious belief that God has somehow alienated a certain amount of His own power, and given it a relative independence of its own; that He has, as it were, set up (relative but still real) obstacles, limits, friction as it were against Himself." This of course, though the Baron apparently did not know it, is nothing but the *Zimzoum* of the Hebrew cabalists which, by underhand channels, had crept into Christian theology. It leads straight on to that dichotomy of the Divine Essence into God the Creator and a pure uncreative Godhead taught by Meister Eckhart and, somewhat illogically, repudiated by Rome. So in one place

(*Essays,* II, 152) you will find him taking his stand with the Church in condemning the plain heresy of Eckhart, and then in the same volume (p. 206) you will find him practically repeating and sanctioning that heretic's plea to rise from the creeping worship of a God to contemplation of the impersonal God-head: "The religious sense, at its deepest and in the long run, will not, must not, be restricted to the Self-limited Creative God, or (worse still) to the persuasion that the whole of the Absolute—that God in and for Himself—has been and is absorbed in God the Creator."

What has happened? Why should theology not remain content with its conception of a God related to the world and grasped in the human experience of religion? Why should it attempt to soar above such a concrete reality to a pure abstraction of reason, and, so attempting, lose itself in vacuity? The answer of the Baron, as of theologians pretty generally, is that the craving for something Absolute is a part of religious experience which demands satisfaction, just as is the "lower" idea of God the Creator, Preserver, and Saviour. There can be no peace for the human soul, no respite from the weariness of all transitory and evanescent pursuits, except through faith in some One Thing fixed and steadfast and immovable, some One Thing utterly unconcerned with the flowing tides of change. In the correspondence, published under the title of *Difficulties,* between Arnold Lunn, then an Anglican, and Ronald Knox, a Roman Catholic priest, I find a bold statement of this need. The Anglican has been arguing for a God somehow limited on the ground that not otherwise can we account for the actual world and leave room for the moral sense of man, and Father Knox cuts through his logic with this drastic assertion of the Absolute:

The point of our difference may be expressed thus. You will not go with me to worship a God who is limited by nothing outside himself, because you do not think that he exists. And I will not go with you to worship a God who is limited by anything outside himself, because I do not care a rap whether he exists or not.

Here would seem to be a radical divergence of a sort to cast suspicion upon the whole inference of theism; but I believe the antinomy has its root in a false terminology, and that some approach to reconciliation might be effected if for the "absolute," the "unconditioned," were substituted the word "ultimate."[2] The difference between these terms, and the consequences of using one or the other, may not be immediately apparent, but will come out by illustration from two of the primary tensions of religion: time and eternity, suffering and impassibility.

Our scholar-saint was much influenced by the Bergsonian philosophy, and in particular by the distinction between so-called clock time and duration. In the former we register a procession of seconds, moments, mechanically following one another like the ticking of a clock, each complete in itself and cut off from its predecessor and successor. That is the character of the succession of events in space, which have no present except as a moving line of division between past and future. But this clock time is quite different

[2] The term "ultimate" I borrow from C. C. J. Webb's insistence in his *Religion and Theism,* on "ultimacy" and "intimacy" as features found in all instances of religion. But I am not at all sure that Professor Webb would accept my distinction between the ultimate and the absolute.

from the durational time of human consciousness. Here the past is not dropped automatically, but is carried on, more or less intact, by memory, while some part of the future also is grasped by anticipation. There is succession from what has been to what is not yet, but succession in the form of a moving present of which past and future are integral parts. The temporal element of consciousness thus carries us along with the procession of broken instants, yet contains also something continuous and consolidative; we are forever multiplied with the tide of things sweeping from past to future, forever one in that composite present which is the seat of the constant Self. Such is the duality of our human state; and, clearly, we measure the strength and depth of the soul just as the continuous element of consciousness usurps upon the flux. The feeble fluttering soul is he who lives most closely to clock time, from moment to moment, untaught by the past, unmindful of the future; whereas the valiant soul is he who lives more completely in durational time. Character grows just with the power to hold the past and the future in the present. To the possessor of character we turn with trust, and from this trust we borrow help and comfort for ourselves under the stress of successive events that beat upon us and are always threatening to disintegrate the solid core of our being.

Here the Ultimate, forever desired and never attainable by man, would be the state of a Being who lives in the succession of time, who has a past and a future, yet to whom no fragment of the past is lost and to whom no possibility of the future is veiled, whose knowledge is eternal though it move in time

with a universe forever flowing and drifting and still
crying out for guidance. Something of the complexity
of human experience, it must be admitted, clings to
the Ultimate so conceived, whereas reason is not content with anything short of absolute simplification.
Hence we see theology pushing intemperately beyond
the Ultimate of faith, and setting up an idol of the
Absolute conceived as an eternity in which there is
no succession, no past or future, but only a static
present spread out in infinite monotony, with no portion in what lies before and after, with no possible
reaction to a world moving in time, severed from life,
alone, self-absorbed in frozen isolation, and to all
human needs perfectly meaningless.

The tension of suffering and impassibility is of the
same nature and springs from the same actuality of
human experience. No man has escaped suffering;
nevertheless, while suffering, we are all of us, in varying degrees, aware of something within us that stands
apart from the passions of life. It is not that we are
so divided as to be two persons, one of which suffers
while the other is impassive, but that there is a duality
reaching in to the centre of consciousness. It is *I* that
feel the pathos, it is *I* that know myself capable of
feeling without loss of personal integrity. Growth in
character, the acquisition of power, again as in the
tension of time, depends on this mastery of suffering, which is a kind of self-mastery. The weak man
is a victim of his passions and a slave of circumstance.
The strong man does not suffer less and is not un-
touched by the depredations of fate—*mentem mor-
talia tangunt*—indeed his capacity for feeling may
grow keener as he rises in manhood; but withal he

is lord of his own soul. Such is the man we trust; that is the pattern of heroism which has inspired the eulogy of poets and sages:

For thou hast been
As one, in suffering all, that suffers nothing.

But this ideal, however we look for it in humanity, however we need it for comfort in our human relations, we nowhere find, neither in ourselves nor in another. And I believe the sheer horror of a universe shaken in every corner of its sentient being by the passions of mutability would drive faith to create for itself, if it could not discover as a reality, an Ultimate analogous to the duality of our experience but without the impotence of human nature. So we have the God of religion: a Being anthropomorphic indeed, as capable of combining *pathos* with impassibility, yet utterly transcendent in the sense that, while responsive to the suffering of a passion-tossed world, His will and purpose are the same from everlasting to everlasting, unalterable amidst all alteration, compassionate yet needing no compassion. We are touching here on a mystery that baffles comprehension; but has any mind ever comprehended the lesser paradox of human personality?

Such is the God whose living reality von Hügel felt, and could make others feel, as did scarcely any one else in his day. Yet again, drawn on by the specious demands of reason, he will solve the ultimate paradox of suffering and impassibility by dropping one of the terms and setting up the other as a pure abstraction. The Infinite shall be removed from the finite as an impassive Absolute: "Religion itself requires the Transcendence of God in a form and a

degree which exclude Suffering in Him." Now in this
our scholar was undoubtedly following the orthodox
view of his Church, and he himself appeals to the
declaration of the Council of Aquileia: *Credo in
Deum impassibilem*. But I believe it may be said with
equal certainty that such a definition arose from an
intrusion of the spurious simplification of metaphysics into the genuine simplicity of the faith. And
it introduces insoluble difficulties into the creed. Its
apparent escape from anthropomorphism means in
truth a denial of personality; though the Baron saw
the peril to theism in any effort to "get rid of the conception of Personality in the Idea of God," as "a *mere*
anthropomorphism, a *pure* myth." It digs an un-
bridgeable gulf between Creator and creature. It
leads inevitably to such a statement as that of Aquinas, which the Baron quotes only to repudiate: "God
enjoys not anything beside Himself, but enjoys Himself alone." And from that it is only a step to the
Absolute of Stoic apathy, as enounced by Epictetus in
what is perhaps the most hideous ideal ever avowed
by philosophy: "It is better that thy son should go to
ruin (*kakon einai*) than that thou shouldst be unhappy."

Von Hügel perceives the chasm of infidelity yawning at the end of the metaphysical path. As a Christian he cannot forget that the God of love must care
for His creatures and, loving, must sympathize with
their suffering; as a pupil of pagan philosophy he will
try to avoid the implications of such an admission by
making a distinction between sympathy and compassion. Which, if it have any sense, means that we ac-
cede in Greek what we retract in Latin. "We must,"

he declares, "beware not to press this [the concession of sympathy] further, so as to mean suffering in God [that is compassion]; for suffering is an evil, and there can be no evil in God [note the ambiguity, as if we should say it is evil for a father to have compassion on his child]."

But it is when he undertakes to reconcile the dogma of the Incarnation with the Absolute of impassibility that the trouble mounts up to anguish. "This poor little shelter of reeds, with the Absolute ever burning down upon it," he cries, "this poor little paper boat, on the sea of the Infinite—God took pity upon them, quite apart from sin and the Fall—God wanted to give their relative independence a quite absolute worth. He took as it were sides with His own handiwork against Himself and gave us the rampart of His tender strong humanity, against the crushing opposition of the pure time- and space-less Eternal and Absolute of Himself." That, evidently, is only another phase of the cabalistic and pseudo-mystic division of the Divine into a God and the Godhead. It is hard enough to reconcile with the text of orthodoxy: "God so loved the world, etc."; for what mockery of fatherhood is this, if the gift was without a pang? And that is but the beginning of the difficulty. What is to be said of the Son who was given so dispassionately by the Father? Surely there was a passion of sacrifice somehow involved in the Incarnation, a passion profound, unfathomable; yet how as God could the Incarnate suffer? To escape that dilemma the Baron invokes the dogma of the two natures. Christ is God and man: in his divine nature he will suffer nothing—nothing at Gethsemane, nothing on Calvary; while his human nature shall be left to undergo the agony alone. That, I protest, is a doctrine psychologically impossible and ethically abhorrent. It is impossible because it so separates a person's "nature" from himself that the nature can go on suffering while the person remains totally unconcerned; it is abhorrent because in effect it turns the whole drama of the Incarnation into something very like a hypocritical farce. It is as if the Son of God pretended to become man and appeared to be like man, sin only excepted, while in reality he—he himself, the person—paid not a farthing of the exacted price. If that be orthodoxy, it is perilously close to the purport of the first formidable heresy of the *Church,* the "docetism" against which the Apostles themselves had to contend. According to this doctrine the Logos did not really take on the nature of humanity, but only "seemed" to do so; Christ the Word condescended to dwell for a while in *a* man Jesus, and then, when the trial came, left the man to endure the penalty of the deception.[3]

It may seem that such a distinction as I have drawn between the Ultimate and the Absolute resembles the

[3] Von Hügel justifies his use of the two-nature dogma by appealing to the Council of Chalcedon. As a matter of fact the content of the actual Definition, in which the Council there assembled gave precision to the Nicean profession of faith, and which ever since has been the foundation rock of Eastern and Western orthodoxy, gives no warrant for hypostatizing one of the natures, so to speak, apart from the personality of the Incarnate. If, elsewhere in their proceedings, the Greek Fathers admitted the impassibility of God in such wise as to attribute the suffering of the Son to his human nature as distinct from his divine nature and his personality, they were led into this error of open docetism and virtual Nestorianism by submission to external authority.

proverbial splitting of a hair; but it is not so. The
difference reaches down to the very heart of the religious life. In the first place to stop with the Ultimate
does not mean that we are presuming to draw an
artificial line about the power of Perfect Goodness,
or to define the essential nature of Deity in terms of
finite understanding; rather it is an honest recognition of the limits of the human mind. Our knowledge
of God ends with what ultimately He is to us and
for us; what, if anything, stretches beyond that the
humanist leaves reverently in the vast unknown.
Pride of intellect belongs rather to those who think
that the Unknowable can be defined in terms of pure
reason. With the bare metaphysician such a presump-
tion may exhaust itself in the innocent abstractions of
a Spinoza or a Kant. For the theist in earnest with his
faith it can have only one logical result: either "complete" mysticism or stark asceticism. In one way or
another as soon as the object of worship is turned
into an Absolute Reality, unconditioned, timeless, im-
passible, severed from the sphere of Appearances by
the gulf of an infinite dualism, just so soon the aim
of religion, if serious, will take the form of reaching
after God by fleeing the conditions of humanity.

It would not be uncharitable to say of most Christians that they live in a middle ground, not of mediation (for indeed there can be no mediation between
the ideal of mediation itself and absolutism), but of
unheroic indecision. The peculiarity of the Baron is
that he was drawn with intense conviction towards
both types of religion, the humane and the metaphysical, having a clear sense of what each of them in
itself implies, yet never seeing their final incompati-

bility. The cost of that intellectual confusion he paid in a wearing strain of the spirit quite different in kind from the normal tensions of life which he understood so well and described so eloquently. Scholar-saint he undoubtedly was; he might have been also the supreme exemplar for our age of religious humanism.

HOW TO READ *LYCIDAS*

AFTER passing, as I might say, through the valley of the shadow of death, after months of physical prostration when reading of any sort was beyond the strength of a depleted brain, the poet to whom I turned instinctively with the first renewal of health was Milton. And so I have been reading Milton again and books about him, with the old zest I had as a boy, and with an added joy of almost tremulous excitement such as a miser might feel at the rediscovery of a treasure of gold stolen from him and long buried out of sight. But with this delight have been mingled certain scruples which vexed me a little more than they did in the old days. Again, as many times before, on laying down one of the poems the familiar words of Tennyson would come unbidden to my mind:

> O mighty-mouth'd inventor of harmonies,
> O skill'd to sing of Time or Eternity,
>   God-gifted organ-voice of England,
>   Milton, a name to resound for ages.

Of the mighty harmonies there would be no doubt; God-gifted voice certainly, organ-voice certainly, for those who have ears to hear. If any one in English, Milton had the divine craft of words, the mastery of sonorous speech. His is not Shakespeare's incalculable gift; it lacks the element of magic that captures us in Shakespeare; it is, or soon after his earliest experiments it was, an art that came by reflection, and as we read him we imagine that we might by equal deliberation attain the same perfection—only we never do attain it. And something of this distinction Milton himself seems to have felt when he wrote of Shakespeare:

> For whil'st to th' shame of slow-endeavoring Art
> Thy easie numbers flow.

The same distinction, I think, was present to Irving Babbitt when he spoke, as I have heard him do more than once, of his experience in quoting. It was Babbitt's custom in the first draught of his essays to cite from memory, and then, before printing, to verify the quotation by reference to the text. He would find occasionally that even his retentive memory had slipped and that he had substituted a word of his own for the poet's. And sometimes, he would say, he could not see that the substitution was inferior to the original—except in the case of Shakespeare. He never made a change in Shakespeare's language but some force or charm was lost. That was not so even with Milton.—Such a difference exists between the seemingly careless spontaneity and the elaborated art of our two supreme masters of poetical diction; and he would be a rash judge who should say that the advantage was all on one side or the other.

But to return to the question that vexed my mood of acquiescent joy. God-gifted organ-voice Milton possessed in full measure—but "voice of England"? Does he speak for the whole of England, or, that being scarcely possible, does he speak from the heart of England, giving articulate expression to that central quality which has made England what we know and love? And by his influence did he maintain that balance and moderation, that sense of law enveloping the individual, which made of Falkland a true type of the Englishman that was to be? Here the question begins with style, but extends beyond mere style to psychology and to principles of government and life.

Now, if there be any hesitation with me to accept Milton's style as the norm of good English, it is certainly not on the ground of that "dissociation of sensibility" which draws a school of modern critics and poets to repudiate what may be called the Miltonic line of development and to seek their parentage in Shakespeare and Donne and the "Metaphysicals." If I understand what the leader of that Choir means by this rather obscure phrase, it is that Milton by conscious choice and judgement dissociated his mind from one whole range of perceptions, refusing to respond to them emotionally as foreign to his fixed theory of values, and by the same deliberate act of selection created a more or less artificial language; whereas the poets proceeding from Donne held their sensibility open to any and every perception and employed words to convey the sharp immediate impression of each fact of sense and experience without discrimination. The distinction is valid, and it is interesting; for the "modernist" in poetry it is of vital significance. But I am not sure that the "dissociation of sensibility," so taken, has been the source of dead monotony and of verbal unreality in our literature; and I am sure that if Milton failed in national leadership it was not for this reason. Rather I should say that his influence in this respect has made for sanity and form and for limitations which are characteristically English. Rather I should maintain that Milton's failure, so far as he failed, was owing to something essentially un-English, or only partially English, to something belonging to his individual temperament, which passed into his philosophy of life and diverted a noble love of liberty into a morbid and isolating passion. Here too Milton was clear-headed in his application of the law to others, but curiously perverse when his own interests were affected. In the second of the sonnets on the book called *Tetrachordon,* he berates his fellow countrymen as "Owles and Cuckoos, Asses, Apes and Doggs" for the very reason that they have lost the true meaning of liberty, while they

> bawle for freedom in this senceless mood,
> And still revolt when truth would set them free.
> Licence they mean when they cry libertie;
> For who loves that, must first be wise and good;
> But from that mark, how far they roave we see
> For all this wast of wealth, and loss of blood.

That is sound doctrine, but—alas to say it!—Milton did not see how apt would be the retort, *de te fabula*; how easy the reply: License he meant when he cried liberty.

This book called *Tetrachordon,* written by Milton himself, was the second of his treatises on divorce, and is a bitter invective against those who, by opposing the facile freedom of marital separation, enslave the soul under man-made laws, forgetting that which "makes us holiest and likest to God's immortal image," and who, for the law of liberty, set up "that which makes us most conformable and captive to civil and subordinate precepts: . . . although indeed no ordinance, human or from heaven, can bind against the good of man." By "the good of man," as Mr.

Tillyard observes in his comment on the passage, Milton means what elsewhere he calls "nature"— damnable word, I add, into which have been distilled all the fallacies of human wit through thousands of years. If you track the word down through its many ambiguities, you will discover that in the end it signifies that which a man temperamentally and personally desires as distinguished from that which is prescribed for him by human rule or divine precept. So it was that Milton, fretted and humiliated because his wife, finding existence with him intolerable, left him and ran away home,—so it was that incontinently he rebelled against the human and divine laws of marriage, and wrote his pleas for freedom of divorce as complying with natural law and the good of man. If ever there was a case of liberty becoming license, it was here. However they may have differed in other respects, in this quality Milton resembled Shelley: they both identified what they desired at any moment with the natural good of man; they both made self-righteousness the law of right.

That was the beginning of Milton's public career and of his prose writings, and it was typical of what ensued. If the bishops in any way interfered with his personal idea of worship, then down with episcopacy and away with the Church; if the monarchical form of government hampered his political independence, then down with monarchy and away with the Constitution. There is no more painful reading in English literature than these apologies for free divorce and regicide which occupied the greatest genius of the age between *Lycidas* and *Paradise Lost,* and the style in which they are written is as heavy and un-English

as their spirit is perverse. There are purple patches
scattered through these treatises, which are all that
most readers know of Milton's prose and which
would give the impression that he is as magnificent
here as in his verse; but if these passages are examined it will be found that, taken apart from their
context, they are expressions of personal ambition,
legitimate in itself and magnificent in its devotion to
the aim of a poet, while all about them floats and
rages a sea of rebellious discontent. I will not endorse
Hilaire Belloc's sweeping condemnation of the prose
works, but in the mass they do certainly form a re-
pellent body of reading. Following the ideas of the
tractates through the surging verbiage, one is reminded of the monsters in the account of creation,
"wallowing unweildie" in

> the vast immeasurable Abyss
> Outrageous as a Sea, dark, wasteful, wilde,
> Up from the bottom turn'd by furious windes.

There is something disconcerting in the spectacle
of a supreme artist, as Milton was in his verse, so
losing his craftsmanship in another medium; what
I would insist on is that the very style of his prose has
a close relation to the fact that when he passes from
imagination to theory his voice is not that of his
people but of an exasperated individual. The seventeenth century, with all its greatness, is an age of
frustration, filled with fine promises that, except in
the field of science, came to no fruition, replete with
noble utterance that somehow failed to convince. In
the Church, in the State, in society, the one thing
needed and not found was a commanding genius that
should have been indeed the voice of England. It is

the tragedy of the time that he who had the genius
so to speak should have wasted his energies in queru-
lous complaints against what was, and in the future
was to show itself, the true spirit of the land. In a
word that spirit may be described precisely as liberty,
not license, as centrality, not dissent.

But I am not concerned to pass judgement on Milton's character and its effect upon his work as a
whole; that is a longer theme than I care now to
discuss. What I started out to do was to consider one
small piece of his output, the *Lycidas,* and to ask
myself how it should be read. To this question, at
least in its acuter form, I was moved by chancing to
take up at the same time Mr. Tillyard's estimation of
the poem and Dr. Johnson's. As a whole I should
regard Mr. Tillyard's *Milton* as about the best book
we have on the man and the poet, a study admirable
for its scholarship and discrimination, and particularly notable for its treatment of the philosophical
problems raised by *Paradise Lost,* such as Milton's
conception of the nature of evil and the cause of man's
fall. Now to Mr. Tillyard *"Lycidas* is the last and
greatest English poem of Milton's youth; though
shorter, it is greater than *Comus,* written with
newly won but complete mastery and expressing a
mental experience both valuable and profound." That
is a sentiment with which my own judgement is in
perfect accord; indeed, I should go further and hold
it to be the greatest short poem of any author in
English, the very criterion and touchstone of poetical
taste. Yet with that opinion I have felt bound to
remember the sweeping condemnation of Johnson, to
whom "the diction" of the poem "is harsh, the

rhymes uncertain, and the numbers unpleasing." It is without passion and without art. In part no doubt Johnson's lack of appreciation can be set down to his known deficiency in the higher faculty of imagination. His comment on the diction and rhythm does nothing more than indicate a certain insensitiveness to the finer and more delicate effects of poetry in general. But one cannot read the whole essay without perceiving that his hostile criticism of the art of *Lycidas* sprang not so much from his miscomprehension and aesthetic obtuseness as from hostility to the poet and to all that Milton as a man stood for. Touching Milton's plea for looser laws of divorce, the neglect of which by the ruling Presbyterians turned him against that sect, Johnson observes, and justly: "He that changes his party by his humour is not more virtuous than he that changes it by his interest; he loves himself rather than truth." As for the political tirades, Johnson in his attack ran true to form: "Milton's republicanism was . . . founded in an envious hatred of greatness, and a sullen desire of independence. . . . He hated monarchs in the State, and prelates in the Church; for he hated all whom he was required to obey. . . . He felt not so much the love of liberty as repugnance to authority." Now for myself I do not like Belloc's summary and contemptuous dismissal of Milton as "a man rotten with the two worst vices: falsehood and pride"; for somehow one shrinks from using such language of a very great poet. To Johnson's charge, on the contrary, I can subscribe without reservation (indeed I have already said much the same thing in weaker language), and I do not see how the charge, in substance, can be countered by any impartial student of Milton's life. But to Johnson the faults of the man were ruinous to the earlier work of the poet, and he denounced *Lycidas* because he read into it the author's ecclesiastical and political heresies; whereas I must reject the maker whilst admiring what he has made. And there the difficulty lies—or has lain for me: how can one so combine detestation and love? how can one make so complete a separation between Milton the destroyer of Church and State, and Milton the artist? how is one to read *Lycidas?*

That particular difficulty, it will be observed, opens up into one of the major problems of criticism in general: the relation between the content of a poem and the art of a poem independent of its content. In the beginning, when that distinction first presented itself to the Greek mind, it took a very simple form and indeed was scarcely a question at all: the *Iliad* and the *Odyssey* were valued primarily, not for their charm and interest, but because in them the statesman, the soldier, the athlete, the man who desired to live honourably, could find the wisest precepts and the best models. For later times, and for us of the West, the principle involved was formulated by Horace in his famous saying that the most successful poet was he who knew how to mix the *utile* and the *dulce*. What Horace meant by the *dulce* is clear enough; it is just that in a poem which gives pleasure to the reader. And what he meant by the *utile* is equally clear; it is that in a poem from which we draw instruction. So in one of the *Epistles* he tells a friend, held in Rome by the practice of declaiming, no doubt about the schools of philosophy, that he is the country reading

Homer, who is a better teacher than all the philosophers:

> *Qui, quid sit pulchrum, quid turpe, quid utile, quid non,*
> *Plenius ac melius Chrysippo et Crantore dicit.*

In exactly that form the question reached the renaissance critics, with the emphasis still heavily on the *utile*. So Puttenham, to name a single example, thinks it necessary to preface his treatise on *The Arte of English Poesie* with a long apology, wherein is shown how "poets were the first priests, the first prophets, the first legislators and politicians in the world," as seen in Homer, Orpheus, Amphion, and the rest. You are back a thousand years and more, and might be reading one of the ancient Greek commentators. But a change came with the advent of the romantic movement. The *utile* and the *dulce* took on new significance, and the old division was sharpened to something like an absolute contrast between two irreconcilable criteria of excellence. The *utile* was broadened so as to embrace the whole substance of a poem whether instructive or not, its sense or meaning. The *dulce* on the other side was refined to a conception of pure poetry, the quintessence of art, as a sort of abstract entity which could be felt and judged somehow apart from any articulate thought or story conveyed; indeed the ideal poem would be a succession of beautiful words with no meaning at all. Such a thesis, baldly stated, is manifestly bare nonsense; but practically the early romantics applied it to criticism by taking *Kubla Khan* as the ideal poem, because, while the content was no more than the shimmering matter of a dream, it reeked of that mysterious entity called pure poetry. And it was not

so long ago that the theory flared up again in France
under the impulse of the Abbé Bremond's monograph
on *La Poésie pure*. The discussion that ensued was
confused by the Abbé's association of aesthetic rap-
ture with a mystical view of the function of prayer.
More illuminating, to me at least, is T. S. Eliot's
pursuit and final rejection of the same ideal of absolute poetry. In his earlier essays, particularly those on
Seneca, Shakespeare, and Dante, you will see him
eagerly pursuing this *ignis fatuus* as the ultimate
standard of value. In the first of those studies he
ranks Shakespeare and Dante together as the supreme
poets of the world, and the two are equally great
though the Italian has taken up into the *Commedia*
the profoundest wisdom of human experience as expounded in the Thomistic theology, whereas the Englishman has no interpretation of life's riddle beyond
the stale platitudes of Seneca. "Perhaps it was Shakespeare's special rôle in history to have effected this
peculiar union—perhaps it is a part of his special eminence to have expressed an inferior philosophy in the
greatest poetry." It is true that Mr. Eliot has his
reservations in supporting this romantic dream of
pure poetry which came to him from certain early
and, as I think, unfortunate associations. It is more
important to note that in his latest enunciation
he has worked himself quite clear of the disturbing
inheritance. There lies before me now his recently
published volume of *Essays Ancient and Modern*,
and in the opening paragraph of one of the "modern"
(that is, hitherto unprinted) essays I am held by this
sentence: "The 'greatness' of literature cannot be determined solely by literary standards; though we must

remember that whether it is literature or not can be determined only by literary standards." That I take to be a complete truth perfectly expressed; and the whole essay on "Religion and Literature" is a masterly application of this sentence to modern currents in verse and fiction. It is the critic come to full maturity after years of probation.

And so, to apply this canon of taste to *Lycidas*, it may be possible for a young man, enamoured of the sheer beauty of words and untroubled as yet by the graver issues of life, to enjoy the marvellous art of the poem with no thought of what the poem means if connected with the poet's place in the world of ideas and action. But such a rupture between the form and the substance of literature cannot long be maintained with the ripening of experience. Sooner or later we are bound to make up our account with that law of taste so ably formulated: "The 'greatness' of literature cannot be determined solely by literary standards; though one must remember that whether it is literature or not can be determined only by literary standards." That *Lycidas* is literature, poetry and not mere verse, depends on the language, the images, the form, on that mysterious working of the imagination which we can feel but cannot ultimately analyse or adequately describe; that it is great literature must depend on the junction of such qualities with nobility of content. And such nobility is there, in full measure.

The poem is an elegy prompted by the drowning of a college friend of the author. It has been the complaint of more than one critic that the expression of grief has little of that warmth which might be expected from such a subject. Dr. Johnson can find no "effusion of real passion, for passion runs not after remote allusions and obscure opinions." Against this charge of frigidity Mr. Tillyard contends with great acumen that the true theme of the poem is not the death of Edward King at all, but the possible death of the poet himself. Milton was writing just before he set out on his voyage to Italy, when such an adventure was more or less perilous and the chance of shipwreck and drowning might very well have occupied his mind. So taken, the charge of coldness towards a friend might be changed to one of cowardice or egotism. But Milton was no coward and, however he may have shown himself elsewhere, the note of egotism is relieved by the artful, though doubtless unconscious transference of anxiety for himself to sorrow for another. And it was not the mere termination of life that made him anxious, but the fear that his one all-absorbing passion might so be left unfulfilled. To understand his state of mind and the emotion that was impelling him to write, the elegy should be read in the light of those passages of self-dedication scattered through his prose works. These purple patches laid upon the coarse cloth of controversy are too well known to need repeating here. The keynote is given by the words inserted in the gross *Apology for Smectymnuus*:

He who would not be frustrate of his hope to write well hereafter in laudable things, ought himself to be a true poem; that is, a composition and pattern of the best and honourablest things; not presuming to sing high praises of heroic men, or famous cities, unless he have in himself the experience and the practice of all that which is praiseworthy.

And joined with this personal ambition was the conviction that no loftier or purer service could be

rendered to one's country and to the world than such
a work as he was preparing himself to produce. Under
the spell of a great heroic poem the mind of the people
would respond in efforts towards great and heroic
living. That was Milton's faith. It was the spirit of
the reformer engrafted upon the temperament of the
artist. In such a profession, wherein personal glory
is identified with public welfare, pride with humility,
there lurks, let us admit, a subtle danger; to fall short
of brilliant success must leave the professor a monu-
ment of ridicule, like the mountains in labour that
brought forth only a mouse. But, on the other hand,
such a purpose, if carried through valiantly to a successful issue, makes the ordinary ambition of the
artist and poet to appear in comparison no more than
a cheap display of vanity. And Milton had the courage
of conviction and the genius to succeed. In the history
of English letters there is nothing like this determination carried through from youth to age, except the
solemn dedication of Wordsworth to a similar purpose. All this must be read into *Lycidas*. Under the
pretext of grief for the loss of a comrade in hope the
poem is in reality as it were the quintessence of those
prose passages through which there speaks a self-
confidence as sublime as it was justified.

It is in the light of this life-long ambition that we
should read the savage attack on the abuses in Church
and State which raises the note of elegy to the "higher
mood" of righteous indignation:

> Last came and last did go,
> The Pilot of the *Galilean* lake. . . .
> He shook his Miter'd locks, and stern bespake,
> How well could I have spar'd for thee, young swain,
> Anow of such as for their bellies sake,

Creep and intrude, and climb into the fold? . . .
But that two-handed engine at the door,
Stands ready to smite once, and smite no more.

And apart from any theory of episcopacy and royalty
the abuses were there and cried out for remedy. Laud
knew them as well as did Baxter, Charles as well as
Cromwell; but none but Milton possessed the "dread
voice" which—alas, but for defects of temper!—
might have done so much to set them right.

In this light also we should interpret the allegorical
symbolism of the poem:

The hungry Sheep look up, and are not fed.

To Dr. Johnson all this masquerade of sheep and
shepherds is "easy, vulgar, and therefore disgusting,"
a cheap device of images without passion and without
art. Johnson had good reason to be suspicious of a
genre that has invited so many weak poets to indulge
in flim-flam. But he should not have forgotten how
all through the Old Testament, from the call that
came to Amos, "who was among the herdmen of
Tekoa," and all through the New Testament, from
the angelic vision that broke upon the shepherds who
were "abiding in the field" about Bethlehem to the
parable that Jesus spake to his disciples, "I am the
good shepherd and know my sheep,"—how all
through the Bible this pastoral allegory of the Church
runs like the very music of religion.

These were the thoughts that haunted the memory
of the poet when he linked himself with his friend as
shepherds:

Together both, ere the high Lawns appear'd
Under the opening eye-lids of the morn,
We drove a field.

Together they were practising their "rural ditties" in preparation for the louder chant that was to stir the nation from its ignoble lethargy, when one of the twain was washed away by the sounding sea, and his voice forever silenced. And what if a like fate awaited the other, who also was about to start on a voyage? "What boots it with incessant care . . . to meditate the thankless Muse," of what avail to "live laborious dayes," when, just as we

> think to burst out into sudden blaze,
> Comes the blind *Fury* with th' abhorred shears,
> And slits the thin spun life?

"But not the praise," he exclaims; the reward and the outcome are not confined to this world nor are they measured by success "on mortal soil," but in heaven before the "witness of all judging *Jove*." I do not know how others are affected, but I can never peruse the climax of the poem without a thrill such as scarcely any other verses of the language excite.

> Weep no more, woful Shepherds weep no more,
> For *Lycidas* your sorrow is not dead,
> Sunk though he be beneath the watry floar,
> So sinks the day-star in the Ocean bed,
> And yet anon repairs his drooping head,
> And tricks his beams, and with new spangled Ore,
> Flames in the forehead of the morning sky:
> So *Lycidas* sunk low, but mounted high,
> Through the dear might of him that walk'd the waves
> Where other groves, and other streams along,
> With *Nectar* pure his oozy Lock's he laves,
> And hears the unexpressive nuptiall Song,
> In the blest Kingdoms meek of joy and love.
> There entertain him all the Saints above,
> In solemn troops, and sweet Societies
> That sing, and singing in their glory move,
> And wipe the tears for ever from his eyes.

Milton always rang true when he wrote of the world to come, but never before nor after did he attain quite this elevation, or achieve so realistic an expression of the invisible mysteries wrapt in the future. A few of his contemporaries possessed this power of giving substance to the hopes of eternity—notably Vaughan—but none of them approaches the master. And in later times the art was simply lost. Choose the best of the moderns, Newman for instance in *The Dream of Gerontius*, and they will appear cold and unconvincing beside Milton. Nor did any of the great poets of the earlier ages of faith quite equal him in this field. I would not compare the few lines of an elegy with the mighty structure of Dante's *Paradiso,* but for myself at least there is no single incident in Dante's voyage through the celestial spheres that touches me with the shock of actuality like that which I feel when I read *Lycidas.* I am not competent to explain by what devices, by what choice of words, Milton obtains his sublime effect. It would be easy of course, if it seemed worth while, to point to the rich manipulation of vowel sounds in this or that verse, to note the startling obviousness of the allusion to the might of him that walked the waves, but the final alchemy of art escapes such an analysis; indeed I question whether any skill of criticism can penetrate to the heart of that mystery of the word which we call inspiration, and leave at that. But one phase of Milton's method impresses me: the fact that his images are borrowed from the simplest commonplaces of faith,—the return of dawn after the sinking of the sun in the ocean stream, the tears wiped away, the heavenly choiring of the blest. A comparison of Newman's attempt to translate the subtler speculations of theology into a poetic account of the soul's awakening after death shows how inevitably right was Milton's choice. There are regions of spiritual experience where the untutored imagination of the people goes deeper into reality than all the groping wisdom of philosophy.

One thing in the end is certain, the "greatness" of *Lycidas* is determined by an intimate marriage of form and matter, expression and substance. He who would read the poem worthily must see this, and must be equally sensitive to the delicacy of its art and to the sublimity of its ideas. This does not mean that he will forget or slur over the disagreeable traits of the poet's character or the repulsiveness of his ecclesiastical and political theories. But for our good fortune what repels us in the man and roused Johnson to a fury of protest is reserved for his prose and is excluded from his poetry—not completely indeed, for, not to mention the more outrageous sonnets, occasionally the bitterness of his disappointed soul breaks out in his later works, yet to such an extent that it is not impossible to keep the poet and the controversialist apart as two almost separate powers. That divorce has its unhappy aspect; for one thing it debars Milton, in his total effect, from being accepted as the voice of England. But it leaves to him the high credit of having raised in *Paradise Lost,* to the honour of his native land, the one monumentally successful product of that humanistic culture of the Renaissance in which originality of genius and faithfulness to the classical tradition are combined in perfect union. And for *Lycidas* there is this further apology, that the elegy was composed before Milton's splendid spirit of liberty was exacerbated by opposition into petulant license, when his personal pride flamed with a yet undiverted zeal to make of his own life a true poem and so to train himself for creating such a work of art as would lift his people from the ugly slough of faction and greed, where they were grovelling, into the finer atmosphere where pure religion and the love of beauty might flourish together.

THE END